D1522639

PRAISES FOR

"ON THE OTHER SIDE

"In our own lives, we have witnessed the power of a simple yes — in the restoration of our marriage and in the birth of our ministry. In this book, Brian Mowrey invites us into a journey of saying yes to God and experiencing "life to the full." Sharing from his own journey of saying yes, he gives practical, relatable and sometimes humorous biblical teaching and illustrations that will encourage you, challenge you and give you a reason to trust the God you can say yes to!"

GREGG AND SHELLEY DEDRICK, FOUNDERS IRON BELL MINISTRIES, FORMER PRESIDENT KENTUCKY FRIED CHICKEN

"'The Other Side of Yes' breathes new life into the often-neglected spiritual disciplines. Brian Mowrey makes this possible through terrific illustrations and applicable Scripture as he beckons his readers to trust God's promises for a better life. Bravo, Brian!"

ROB STRONG, SENIOR PASTOR GRACE COMMUNITY CHURCH AND AUTHOR OF "THE BIG GUY UPSTAIRS"

"Brian Mowrey invites his readers to say yes to the most important journey of their lives. Though he may never have met you, you will hear and see yourself clearly in many of his stories. Filled with practical steps and biblical truths, Brian offers a simple yet transformational plan to becoming more the person God created you to be while changing the ordinary into the extraordinary. If you are looking to leave regret behind and live a life of exhilarating purpose, this book will absolutely illuminate the path to getting there."

NIRO FELICIANO, LCSW, PSYCHOTHERAPIST AND HOST OF THE "ALL THINGS LIFE" PODCAST

"It's well-known among people in the industry that a healthy dose of cynicism is part and parcel with being a TV comedy writer and standup comic. But Brian Mowrey's storytelling is transformative and warm. He's funny without trying — which pains me to say — and he shares of himself with ease and wit and kindness. 'On the Other Side of Yes' is encouraging and triumphant — a balm to my slightly disillusioned soul."

TIM WASHER, CONTRIBUTOR TO SATURDAY NIGHT LIVE, THE LATE SHOW, CONAN AND LAST WEEK TONIGHT WITH JOHN OLIVER

"Leaning forward and saying yes to challenges is Brian Mowrey's signature. Now he has unpacked his personal motivation so that every reader can be pulled toward joyful and fresh obedience to Christ. If I have learned anything in four decades of pastoring, it is that just trying harder to say 'no' to habits and sins will never succeed until a greater 'yes' pulls a person toward a new horizon. This book will give you a host of proactive goals and courageous pioneers to help you say yes to the living voice of God in your life."

ROGER THOMPSON, TEACHING PASTOR BEREAN BAPTIST CHURCH

"This book should be required reading for anyone who wants to live life to its fullest potential. It's an invitation to awaken your faith, recenter your focus on the things that matter most and, most importantly, align yourself with God's will for your life. Say yes!"

JESSICA REINHART, ENTREPRENEUR AND FOUNDER OF LUMITORY

"Brian Mowrey takes us on a journey to a life of abundance, blessing and freedom in this practical, witty and compassionate book. A powerfully convicting read that not only creates a hunger for godly transformation but also a deep desire to do whatever is necessary to pursue it. At a time in our world where there's so much unrest, uncertainty and division, this book lays out so beautifully how saying yes to God is for everyone for such a time as this."

CARRIE L. AMOS, LCSW, PRESIDENT JERICHO PARTNERSHIP

"Brian's friendship is an example of the truth lived out through the words he writes. In the span of the seven and a half years since my baby girl died, Brian has been steadfast in remaining alongside our family — never shaken by the silence, rattled by the questions or surprised by the comments we make. His laughter, gentle assurance, concern, care and compassion are beacons that have guided me through the murky waters of grief to a life lived fully and in abundant joy on the other side of yes."

JENNY HUBBARD, PRESIDENT CATHERINE VIOLET HUBBARD FOUNDATION

ON THE

step out

OTHER

catch the wind

SIDE OF

brace for adventure

YES

BRIAN MOWREY

To request permissions, contact hello@brianmowrey.com.

Paperback: ISBN 9798671479850

First paperback edition: August 2020

Edited by Anna Mae Althen
Cover art and layout by Parker Hu

Printed by Kindle Direct Publishing in the USA.

TO BECCA

SO THANKFUL

COMPLETELY OVERJOYED

AND BEYOND BLESSED

THAT YOU SAID YES

"I used to think you had to be special for God to use you, but now I know you simply need to say yes."

BOB GOFF, "LOVE DOES: DISCOVER A SECRETLY INCREDIBLE LIFE IN AN ORDINARY WORLD"

CONTENTS

INTRODUCTION

GOODBYE MAYBE, HELLO YES

God's best for you is on the other side of your yes to Him. This has always been the case. Mountains move on the other side of fully trusting God's call on our lives. The stories of the Bible would be drastically different if the characters all said no. Imagine if Abraham didn't believe or if Mary said, "Find another surrogate." Moses could have thrown water on the burning bush or, even worse, decided to put it out in a more manly way. (Just to be clear, I'm thinking of a fire extinguisher.) Imagine if Moses didn't have the guts to believe God would do something if he put his staff in the water. What if the disciples refused to drop their nets or if the little boy with the bread and fish said, "These are mine," and refused to give them up? What if the wedding reception staff told Mary they didn't need her son's help? They would have all been drinking water the rest of the night. Thankfully, they all said yes. God moved powerfully on the other side of their yes, and we know them as world changers today.

This book is about the transformational power of saying yes to God.

It's about stepping into a more vibrant and exciting life following and serving the Lord. It's about trusting God and being ready to say yes to Him no matter what. This book will give you the tools to step past the things that have always prevented you from saying yes.

For me, one of the most graceful things to watch is hang gliders soaring high in the sky. There is such beauty looking at the vibrant colors as they float across the horizon. I've always imagined it being very peaceful soaring in midair beneath the strong wings of a hang glider. But before enjoying the ride, the hang glider had to jump. They had to say yes to the journey. They had to trust the strength of the wind. This is what it's like to be a follower of Jesus. It is the most grace-filled and exhilarating life you could possibly live. But you have to jump. You have to say yes to the journey, and you must trust the strength of God's presence to carry you.

Growing up playing hockey, I had the joy of meeting all kinds of characters. One summer, I spent a week in Boston at a hockey camp. I joined 20 other players from across New England. One of the players was a guy named Marty. On the first day, all the guys were sizing each other up, trying to claim their rightful position in the pee wee hockey camp ranks. Marty had a particularly aggressive strategy. He came into the locker room and announced to the entire room, "I'm Marty. I'm in charge. And if you don't like it, I'll take on any of you anytime, anywhere." Under most circumstances, this would have been a soul-shaking moment harkening enormous fear within each of our skinny middle school bodies. However, in this case, it led to loud uncontrollable laughter. If you were imagining the booming voice of James Earl Jones coming from Marty, you made a casting error. Think Cindy Lou Who. And if you were picturing a strong intimidating bully, you would be wrong again. Instead, picture Mr. Burns from the Simpsons. Not surprisingly, none of us were very intimidated. Yet, I'll never forget his bold words, "Anytime, anywhere." And I knew he meant it. The question is, do we? Are we ready to say yes to the Lord anytime, anywhere?

For 10 years, my buddy, whom I affectionately call Crazy Craig, to the best of his ability, has committed to saying yes to the Lord anytime, anywhere with and for anyone. This commitment has led him on fascinating adventures. Why? Because when we step out and trust the Lord, He always shows up. Saying yes is what it means to partner with the Lord. We often think we must know everything, be ready for everything and be equipped for everything before saying yes to anything. Yet, this is not how our walk with the Lord works. Part of our commitment to saying yes must be a willingness to get it wrong. The disciples were professional fishermen, not professional leaders, healers or communicators. Their part was saying yes, and God did the rest.

One day, Crazy Craig took his kids to a pet store to see the animals. While there, he noticed one of the workers who was over the top grumpy. This worker was giving Craig and his family the coldest of shoulders. Fighting back the urge to return what he was receiving, Craig remembered his commitment to say yes anytime, anywhere. And of course, this was one of those moments the Lord asked him to prove it. If we make a commitment to say yes, God is going to challenge us. Craig noticed that this worker had injured her arm. As she worked, it was clear that she was in pain. Craig and his kids approached the grumpy woman and said, "Excuse me. We noticed that you are in pain. Can we ask what happened? Are you ok?" Her eyes softened. The woman couldn't believe that this family cared. She opened up that her shoulder was in pain and thanked them for caring. Her whole demeanor changed. Then the Lord asked Craig to do something uncomfortable — pray for her. He said yes. He asked her if they could pray for her. To their surprise, she said yes. After they prayed, Craig asked if she felt any better. Guess what? She did. She asked them to pray for her headache as well, so they did.

That is exactly what it means to follow Jesus — to live a "so they did" life. In the book of Acts, the story of Philip and the Ethiopian is told. In this story, Philip meets an Ethiopian dignitary, has the opportunity to ride in a carriage, baptizes said Ethiopian and teleports to another city. How does this all happen? It all starts with Philip's radical yes. The story begins with an angel of the Lord calling Philip to walk south down a desert road and walk alongside a carriage. It would have been easy for Philip to say, "I'm too busy" or "South is out of my way." Instead he says yes, and he gets the chance to see and experience the power of God. In fact, all Scripture says about Philip's yes is, "So he started out." He was asked, so he started out. The Lord called him, and he said yes.

We live in a maybe world when God is calling us to respond with a resounding yes. I've found it increasingly difficult to get people to respond to anything these days. I coach U7 girls' soccer and it is nearly impossible to get anyone to help. Hopefully, if they read this book, they will be guilted into saying yes to signing up for snacks. This Saturday is open by the way. Surprisingly, I discovered that an effective way to get a response from people is through an evite. I didn't understand why until I finally figured it out. It's because you can respond to the evite with a maybe. The options are yes, no or maybe – and everyone loves to check maybe. This reflects our culture today. We love to check maybe. We love keeping our options open for something better to come along. Checking maybe is saying, "I see your invitation. It has potential. But I'm holding out for something better. Maybe I'll see you there." Friends, when it comes to our faith, it's time to say goodbye to maybe and hello to yes. The Lord is not looking for a maybe. He is searching the earth for those who will have the courage to say yes to Him anytime, anywhere.

I truly believe that a deeper walk with the Lord and a more vibrant and exciting faith are on the other side of your yes. This book is split into three sections, each focusing on an important aspect of saying yes to the Lord. The first section focuses on saying yes to the promises of God. This is a necessary first step. Before saying yes to the call of God in our lives, we must first respond to His promises about who He is and who He has made us to be. The second section focuses on saying yes to devotion. We have been created to be in relationship with the Lord, and He has given us ways to grow in our relationship. In this section, I will challenge us to say yes to things like prayer, forgiveness, gratitude and compassion. Through these disciplines, God has given us the keys to grow in our relationship with Him. The third section focuses on saying yes in every season. Saying yes to the

Lord is not determined by our circumstances. Instead, saying yes to the Lord is a good decision in any season. Specifically, I will speak to the need to say yes in a season of waiting, a season of suffering and a season of celebration.

One yes fed 5,000. One yes rebuilt the temple. One yes parted a sea. One yes led to walking on water. One yes led to becoming the mom to a very special child. One yes can change the world. Imagine what might be on the other side of your yes.

SECTION 1

SAY YES TO HIS PROMISES!

"Behold, I am with you and will keep you wherever you go, and will bring you back to this land. For I will not leave you until I have done what I have promised you." **GENESIS 28:15**

Saying yes to the Lord starts with saying yes to His promises. It would be irresponsible to say yes to someone you were unsure you could trust. Equally, it would be unwise to say yes to something that would greatly impact your life if you didn't know it was for your good. As the father of four girls, my daughters say yes to me (just pretend it's true) because they know they can trust me, and they know what I teach them and what I ask of them is ultimately for their good. Stepping into the "say yes" lifestyle with the Lord starts with a deep understanding of who God is and how He sees us. Our life of saying yes to the Lord is on the other side of encountering the reality that His promises are true. In this section, I invite you to say yes to three promises made to you by God that will set you free into an adventurous life following and serving the Lord.

CHAPTER ONE
YOU ARE LOVED

"'Though the mountains be shaken and the hills be removed, yet my unfailing love for you will not be shaken nor my covenant of peace be removed,' says the Lord, who has compassion on you." **ISAIAH 54:10**

When my wife Becca was young, her parents took the whole family to Disney World. My father-in-law tells the story about walking down Main Street in the Magic Kingdom. He was holding the hand of one of his daughters, Kathleen. She was 5 at the time. As Ken was walking, hand-in-hand with Kathleen, he noticed that people were staring at him. He wondered why but kept on walking. Then he noticed the scowls grew more condemning, with even more people shaking their heads at him in disgust. He thought, "What's going on? Why are these complete strangers so put off?" Then he looked down at little Kathleen.

His little angel blissfully glided along with her father with her right hand grasping his, and her left hand clinging to a cigarette she had picked up off the street that she pretended to smoke. To those passing by, it appeared Kathleen was taking a smoke break between rides — with her father's full approval. After Ken recovered from his shock, he quickly exchanged the cigarette with an oversized and overpriced Mickey Mouse-shaped lollipop, non-filtered.

So many of us carry around things we shouldn't — shame, hurt, regret. You might be carrying a lie that was spoken over you or holding on to a past mistake that you have allowed over time to define you. You might be carrying a heavy load of stress or an outdated vision from the past. Is it a dream that needs to be laid down or a view of yourself that is too low or, worse, too high? What are you carrying around, and where did you get it from? Is it from the Lord or a toxic temptation that someone else discarded?

The unconditional love of God is the greatest gift you will ever receive. Saying yes in this chapter will launch you into a life-changing adventure — one I affectionately call "The Great Exchange," whereby we allow the Lord to remove the toxins, lies and failures and exchange them for His abounding love.

But why is God giving us this gift? Have you ever questioned the motivation behind a gift that was given to you, or have you suspected a hidden agenda? What was the person's motive when he or she complimented you, asked you that question or gave you that present? Could it be that the gift giver wants something from me in return? Perhaps the gift is not really a gesture of affection and thoughtfulness but instead an obligation. Knowing the motivation of the gift giver is just as important as what's under the wrapping.

Sometimes gifts are marked with an asterisk – they are conditional. The offering of a home-cooked meal doesn't taste as good when you're suspicious there might be a baited hook lurking inside the pot roast. Why am I sharing this? In Scripture, we learn that God gives us wonderful gifts.

The gift of every breath.

The gift of family and friends. Well, most of them.

The gift of His creation.

The gift of forgiveness.

The gift of His presence.

The gift of eternal life. Just to name a few minor ones.

So, what was God's motivation behind giving us these gifts? Why has God blessed us? These are important questions because how you answer them will determine how you view God. And how you view God influences what you believe about yourself and the world around you.

The answer to these weighty questions is found in the most famous Bible passage of all time. You know, the one the circus clown is always holding in the endzone of almost every nationally televised football game – John 3:16: "For God so loved the world that He gave His one and only Son, that whoever believes in Him shall not perish but have eternal life." God's motivation for everything is love.

God loves us.

God loves you.

You are not a mistake.

You are not forgotten.

You are not unlovable.

You are loved by God.

God has given us a promise – the best promise, the greatest gift. And we have a choice to say YES to receiving it, to exchange what we are carrying for what He has to offer. We shouldn't be satisfied with anything less than the love of God. This is a call to look up and see the extent of God's love for you.

Every summer, our family has been blessed with the opportunity to vacation at a beautiful lake house owned by one of our good friends. It's a highlight for us each year. One of the things we love to do is go to the arcade. I know, beautiful scenery all around us and we choose to spend our time competing for the highest score on Space Invaders. In case you were wondering, the town of Laconia, New Hampshire boasts one of the largest arcades in the United States — or at least that's what their sign says. And it's right next to the coffee shop with the world's best coffee. Imagine that! My four girls love to win tickets so they can go to what I call the most stress-filled square feet on the planet – the prize counter. My wife Becca has superpowers, so she can brave this level of tension. As for me, I usually play Skee-Ball while she negotiates with the half-asleep high schooler "working" the counter.

One year was particularly exciting when a man gave us all his tickets. And when I say all his tickets, I mean over twenty thousand tickets. To this day, we call him the Arcade Angel. My kids had never even dreamed about that many tickets. Years of cashing in paltry winnings had conditioned my daughters to see only the bottom shelf of prizes, and they began their search for the perfect finger puppet, Dora the Explorer eraser and edible crayon, all appraised in the two to four ticket range. I thought to myself, "In order to dodge this entire arbitration, I'll be stuck playing Skee-Ball until next Tuesday, and I don't have the coin to finance that level of conflict avoidance." So, I decided to step in and help. "Girls," I said "The Ticket Angel gave you twenty thousand tickets. You no longer have to pick from the bottom shelf. Look up!" They didn't realize it, but with their inheritance they could now choose from the cherished fortune perched on the top row with the life-sized stuffed pandas. Once they comprehended the magnitude of the gift they had been given, their eyes lit up. They couldn't believe they had access to such treasure.

For much of my walk with the Lord, I was picking from the bottom shelf, not knowing that I had been given access to so much more.

I knew God loved me, but I never sought to experience the extent of His love. My knowledge of His love stayed on the bottom shelf. Logically I knew the Bible taught that God loved me, but I hadn't explored and encountered the multiple dimensions of His love. I wonder, when it comes to the love of God, do you need to look up? We have been given an invitation into knowing and experiencing the fullness of God's love.

In the book of Ephesians, the Apostle Paul prays over the church in Ephesus, "And may you have the power to understand, as all God's people should, how wide, how long, how high, and how deep his love is" (Ephesians 3:18). I've so often read over these words and thought to myself, "Paul is telling us that God's love is big – I get it." However, Paul doesn't just say, "God's love is big." No! He says that he wants us to grasp the fullness of God's great love. God's love is not just big; it is wide, long, high and deep. It is vastly bigger than big!

There is a great story in Genesis Chapter 13 about Abraham. God made Abraham a promise that, through him, a great nation would be birthed. So many people would come from the line of Abraham that he would not be able to count them. It would be like counting each grain of sand at the beach or every star in the sky. God would also bless him with land. Abraham would have to wait many years to see this promise fulfilled. Finally, God brought Abraham into his inheritance and commanded him to "walk through the land in the length of it and in the breadth of it" (Genesis 13:17).

He was told to take a walk.

God wanted Abraham to know every square inch of the land. Imagine him walking from corner to corner examining what the Lord had so graciously given him. Think of the plants he discovered, the animals that made their home in his land and the fruit that could be picked. God wanted him to become an expert on his inheritance.

Friends, we have an inheritance as well. It's the love of God, and the Lord is calling us to survey and experience the length and breadth of it. The question is, will we take the walk? Will we examine every square inch?

God's love is wide, long, high and deep.

GOD'S LOVE IS WIDE ENOUGH TO EMBRACE EVERYONE.

In my yard, there is a rock that I always mow around. The rock is right in the middle of the lawn. One day, I decided I was going to dig up the rock so that I could plant grass. Once I began digging, I quickly discovered that what I thought was a small rock was actually a medium-sized rock. So, I kept digging.

Update: It was a large-sized rock. More digging.

An extra-large-sized rock.

Plymouth Rock.

Rock of Gibraltar.

As it turns out, the mantle layer of the earth begins in my backyard.

As I continued digging, I found that the rock in my backyard was immovable. This is even more true of the love of God. His love is immovable. Its span is immeasurable. It's unconditional. His love does not change based on your feelings or behavior. You might think you are not standing in the love of God, that somehow His love is not wide enough to reach around you. But the truth is, you can't fall outside the love of God. It's wide enough to embrace everyone. That means you!

GOD'S LOVE IS LONG ENOUGH TO NEVER RUN OUT.

In a love-runs-out culture, the reality that God's love never runs out is a difficult concept to grasp. Beloved athletes chase contracts and abandon our favorite teams. Our favorite song is replaced within months. The picture you love only lasts 10 seconds on Snapchat. There it is; now it's gone. Our favorite shows are binge watched and forgotten. Friends often fail us and hurt us. Jobs are not dependable. And sadly, we live in a world where the American Psychological Association has reported that 40-50% of all first-time marriages end in divorce. We are not expecting love to last because we seldom experience lasting love. Yet, this is the love of God. His love is long enough to never run out. There is nothing you could do to shorten it. His love will never wear out, thin out or run out. Everything else in this world may fail us, but the love of God never will.

GOD'S LOVE IS HIGH ENOUGH TO SEE PAST ANY OBSTACLE.

One of my family's favorite stores is TJ Maxx. You know, the one where nothing is where it's supposed to be. One afternoon, while perusing through the store, my youngest daughter Bria stumbled upon a stuffed animal deer in the candle isle ... she had to have it. Carrying the newly beloved animal around the store, she launched into the famous speech all children learn at an early age, "This is all I want. It's all I need." And then my favorite, "Papa, I promise, I'll never ask for anything ever again." Somehow, in her little mind, she believed that, if she had this stuffed animal, all would be right in the world. This one-of-a-kind stuffed deer would fulfill her every desire. Happiness and contentment would be forever found.

Like Bria, I think we often buy into this belief.

If I could just get that.

Have this.

Be there.

All will be well with my soul.

There exists in the hearts and minds of every human a lifelong hunger for fulfillment and satisfaction. We believe there must be something out there that if found, all would be well. So, we search the earth for the thing that will make us content and complete, the thing that will satisfy our souls. Here is the good news. God has it and wants to give it to you. It's His love. When we experience the love of God, we discover it was the one thing we have been missing. It's the one thing that satisfies us and brings a sense of completeness. We awaken to the reality that the love of God is what we have been searching for the whole time. And when you encounter the love of God, you are lifted to a height that allows you to see past any obstacle. It becomes the one thing that can never be taken from you. The love of God becomes the thing you can always stand on. And when you stand on the love of God, you can see past any obstacle.

A scary health journey looks different when you know the love of God.

An uncertain future looks different when you know the love of God.

A hurtful word looks different when you know the love of God.

A step of faith looks different when you know the love of God.

The love of God changes everything!

THE LOVE OF GOD IS DEEP ENOUGH TO MEET US IN EVERY NEED.

God's love is not intimidated by your issue. God's love is not left wondering what to do in your time of need. His love is deep enough to meet you in any season and in any situation.

When I met Al, he had just come out of prison. This was not a guy you wanted your kids to meet. He had been in and out of prison more times than he could count. He got himself involved in a prominent gang because they helped him score heroin. He now owed them. The gang leaders used that leverage to get Al to do little jobs for them, usually robbing stores and stealing from citizens on the streets of Minneapolis. This led to bigger jobs. Al became a messenger for the leaders of the gang. This meant sending people who owed the gang money "messages" that would compel them to pay up. He was the enforcer. He once told me that, on any given week, he would send five to 10 people to the intensive care unit of the hospital. If you owed the gang money and you got a visit from Al, you would have seven days to heal and one day to pay them back. Al was a bad guy.

When I met Al, he had just entered a drug rehabilitation program. He finally wanted to get his life right. The program required the guys to attend church on Sunday. Al liked coming to my church because we met in the evening, which meant he could sleep in. For several months, Al had been coming to our church services, but he hadn't decided to become a Christian. One evening after service, Al was sitting in one of the chairs with his head pressed into his hands. I sat next to him. Not sure what to say, finally I asked, "Al, are you alright?" He looked up at me and began to tell a story. When he was a kid, Al's brother tried to teach him how to dive. The problem was, when his brother was teaching Al to dive, he forgot to check the depth of the lake. Al stood on the edge of the dock, hung his hands over his head and his brother helped him fall into the water. Without knowing, Al dove into about three feet of water. He was rushed to the hospital where it would take multiple surgeries and hours of rehabilitation for Al to relearn to walk. Then Al looked up at me and asked, "Pastor Brian, how can I be sure the love of God is deep enough for me?"

Al was wondering if the love of God was deep enough to cover His sins. He was wondering if there was enough in the love of God to take on his shame and guilt, face to face. He was wondering if the supply of God's love was full enough to minister to his level of brokenness. Al wanted to know, when placed on the scale, which would outweigh the other — God's love or his sin? Before diving in, he wanted to know if the love of God could hold him.

I want to tell you friends that the love of God is deep enough to meet you in every season and in every circumstance. There is no shallow end to the love of God. In His love, God will forgive every sin, wipe away all shame, minister through any season. His love will not back down to your trouble or become anxious facing the thing that overwhelms you. God's love is deep enough to meet us in every need. Al encountered the love of God that day. He now serves as a chaplain for an inner-city ministry in Minneapolis, telling everyone about the depth of God's love.

God loves you. Will you say YES to this promise? Will you trust that God loves you and begin to wholeheartedly seek to understand how wide, how long, how high and how deep His love is for you? Will you say YES to carrying His love wherever you go?

Your treasure is waiting for you. All you have to do is look up!

CHAPTER TWO
YOU HAVE A PURPOSE

"But you are a chosen people, a royal priesthood, a holy nation, God's special possession, that you may declare the praises of Him who called you out of darkness into His wonderful light." **1 PETER 2:9**

Why are we here? It's an important question. Life is empty without purpose. You can have a full bank account and still feel empty. You can have a full resume and still be wandering. You can have a full house but an empty heart. Friedrich Nietzsche once said, "He who has a why to live for can bear almost any how." Simon Sinek captured the world when he gave his TED talk, "Start With Why." Simon retaught the world that a great leader can answer the why question. Why are we doing what we are doing? Not only is this essential for great leaders, but answering the why question is essential for every human being. Why are you here?

There was a man of God in the Bible named Elijah. He had a habit of listening to the Lord. God told him to move to a town called Zarephath, so he did. God told him to challenge a group of prophets, so he did. And the Lord heard Elijah as well. Elijah asked God to raise a boy back to life, and He did. The Lord was clearly using Elijah in powerful ways. You would never think a guy like Elijah would question his purpose for living, but he did.

A woman named Jezebel threatened Elijah's life, so he ran. And he ran far. For 40 days and 40 nights, Elijah ran away. He was like the Forest Gump of the Bible. Finally, he made it to a cave on Mount Horeb. Here, God met him and spoke to him. God loved Elijah so much that He went to him, even though he was in the wrong place. This is what God does for us as well. And then the Lord asked Elijah, "What are you doing here, Elijah?"

We have all asked this question, maybe even today. It's not just about physical location. It's a question about purpose. Elijah, why are you in this place? Personalize it. What are you doing here, Brian? What are you doing here (your name here)? Why are we here?

I'm so grateful that the Lord has given us an answer to this question. We have been made on purpose for a purpose. We have a high calling and an important mission. This chapter is all about saying yes to our purpose. I'd like to share three challenges with you. The first is to say yes to your God-given purpose. The second is to say yes to your unique calling. And the third is to say yes to God's equipping.

CHALLENGE NO. 1: SAY YES TO YOUR GOD-GIVEN PURPOSE.

The book of Exodus is the story of God delivering His people Israel from their Egyptian oppressors. God called Moses from a burning bush to deliver His people out of captivity. There are many amazing things about this story, but one of them is that the Lord reveals our purpose for being on earth. Six times the Lord tells Moses to go to Pharaoh and say, "Let my people go, so that they may worship me."

"So that they may worship me."

I love that God doesn't just give the command; He gives the why. The command is to let His people go. And the reason was so that they could worship Him. Imagine the story if it went like this:

Moses: "The Lord told me to tell you, 'Let my people go.'"

Pharaoh: "Why?"

Moses: "Just let His people go."

Pharaoh: "Why?"

Moses: "I'm not sure. I'll go find out."

God gives the command. He wanted His people to be free. He still does. Then God gave the reason why — so they could worship Him. This reveals our purpose. It's to worship the Lord. We have been set free to worship Him. I always wondered why God came to earth as an infant. Why didn't He show up on the scene as a man in his twenties?

He could have avoided the awkward teenage years filled with peer pressure and pimples. God must have been very intentional about entering our world as an infant. You see, if Jesus came as a young adult, the wise men may have come with all their questions. The shepherds may have come with all their complaints. And maybe this is how we enter the presence of God today. But as an infant, the only thing they could do was bow down and worship. They could have asked Him questions, but they would have gotten no response. They could have brought their complaints or suggestions, but the infant wouldn't have cared. So, all they could do was bow down and worship. Even at His birth, Jesus was leading people into their purpose.

So, if our purpose is to worship the Lord, then what is the purpose behind that purpose? Why is worshipping the Lord so important?

First, worshipping the Lord is important for our well-being. To worship the Lord means to live for the Lord every day. It means putting Him first in our lives. We worship the Lord when we listen to Him, much like Elijah did, and the Lord knows that the best life for us comes from choosing to listen to Him. In this moment, you might say, "I don't want to listen to anyone." Good luck with that. Reality is, we are always listening to someone. It could be a trusted mentor, a famous icon, a sitcom that informs our humor or a politician who influences our convictions. And if nobody else, then we are left listening to ourselves. We are always listening to someone. The question is, "Who are you listening to?" God's call to worship Him is a call to listen to Him. This is where a life with purpose begins. And it is for our good.

When was Elijah thriving the most?

In the cave?

Or while listening to the Lord?

As you read about his story in the Bible, you will quickly realize his greatest adventures were found on the other side of listening to the Lord. He found that his best life was on the other side of yes.

Second, worshipping the Lord is important because it's how we participate in God's mission for the world. There is no greater work than to be working into the mission of God. I love Rick Warren's opening line in his book, "A Purpose Driven Life," which says, "It's not about you." This is so true. In 2018, Google statistics reported over 93 million selfies were taken every day. This is a problem — but not a new one. Even the disciples were thinking about themselves as they vied for the best spot in the afterlife. Although they could not take a selfie, they might as well have. They were self-focused. And when we focus on ourselves, we miss our purpose in this world. When we worship, we take the attention off our self and place it on the Lord and enter the mission we have been sent to accomplish.

Let me take you back to where this self-focused problem began. Before God created humankind, the angels existed (Job 38:4-7). There was one angel who was chief of them all, and his name was Lucifer. This high angel became jealous of God and wanted to be just like Him (Isaiah 14:12-16). In his free will, Lucifer rebelled against the

Lord. Because of this rebellion, the Lord cast Lucifer from Heaven to earth (Luke 10:18-20). Lucifer set up camp on earth to worship his selfie! Within this context, Adam and Eve appeared on the scene. They walked with God and worshipped Him. Through their fellowship with God, they would bring something new to the earth – they would bring light into darkness. The intention all along was to expand the garden (Gen. 1:28), snuff out the darkness and restore the brokenness caused by Satan. This has become our mission today. And it happens through worship. Later, Jesus would tell His disciples, "You are the light of the world" (Matt. 5:14). And this is our purpose – to be the light of the world, to restore what is broken and to flood out the darkness with light. And it all happens when we live a life worshipping the Lord.

CHALLENGE NO. 2: SAY YES TO YOUR UNIQUE CALLING.

There's this kid at our church who is an excellent drummer. He wasn't always excellent. But he worked at it and now every time he plays, he kills (music lingo for he does well – I think). I can walk into the room and know it's him playing without even looking. He has found his unique style and sound that set him apart. He's discovered his unique way of shining. He's found his groove. Our purpose on this planet is to play our part in worshipping the Lord with our lives. We all need to find our unique groove.

The Apostle Paul talks about this in his letter to the church in Corinth. He says that together we form the body of Christ. Each of us represents a different part of the body. Each part is important and useful to the whole. And each part was created to work alongside the other parts. And the part that might seem like the weakest is just as important.

I sometimes play in a men's hockey league. It's what we call adult gym class. During one game, I took a slap shot off my skate. It hit me right on top of the laces. I played the rest of the game (because I'm tough) and then took my skate off to discover black and blue toes. I had broken two of my toes. Up until then I never thought about my two little toes. They didn't seem that important. But they do now. Today I can tell you how important those two little toes are. It gave me a fresh understanding of the importance of each body part. All of us are important and have an essential part to play in the body of Christ.

Which begs the question, "How do we find our groove?" If our purpose is to worship the Lord and to bring light into the darkness, then we need to find our unique calling within that purpose. How does that happen? Let me offer three suggestions.

First, we can discover our unique calling through study. When we study God's Word, one of the privileges is discovering how God has called and worked through others in the past. You get to see how God used Aaron, Deborah, Lydia, Peter, Priscilla and David. Each of them was empowered by God to do great things. By studying their lives, we can be inspired by the ways the Lord wants to empower us.

Second, we can discover our unique calling by stepping out in faith and evaluating the results. Finding your groove will not happen by sitting on the couch. Discovering the way God wants to shine light through you will most likely happen as you step out in faith. Leave the blocks. Get out of the gate. Start serving and then evaluate. After stepping out in faith, ask yourself, "What is God blessing? Where do I see the fruit?" Allow your spiritual gift to find you as you live out your faith.

Third, we can discover our unique calling through the counsel of others. So often it's been the words of others that have directed me into the places and positions that God had for me. The wisdom of others is invaluable. All of us need a handful of people we can turn to for counsel. These should be people who you look up to because of their faith in the Lord and people who want what is best for you and won't be afraid to tell you the hard stuff. Invite them to speak into your life.

Once you find your groove – play and play often. It will take time to learn your part.

My daughter Norah loves robots. We bought her one for her birthday. Guess what happened when we pulled it out of the box? Nothing. It was just a bag of parts. We spent the next several weeks putting it together, testing and adjusting as needed. The gifts of God are similar. Perhaps they should come with an inscription, "Some assembly required." God blesses us with gifts that require developing. Saying yes to your purpose means saying yes to finding your unique calling. What's your groove?

CHALLENGE NO. 3: SAY YES TO GOD'S EQUIPPING.

When I was in college, I was in a band. (Don't look it up. We weren't very good.) On one of our trips, we found ourselves in Montana playing at a youth conference. We stayed in a friend's house. Mr. Joe was a pastor and a rancher, which I discovered is the case for nearly every person in Montana. Everyone has a job, and they also work on a ranch, or so it seems. Rancher Joe told us he needed our help one day. He had a great mission for us. He needed us to help him get the cattle from a pasture to a small pen. He put me in charge of the gate at the pen. My job was simple. Open the gate when the cattle came down the hill and close it once they were inside. He also told me I would need to direct the cattle into the pen. For this task, he gave me a tennis racket. Mind you, I have no experience as a rancher or a tennis player. Then Mr. Joe got on his four-wheeler and shouted, "I'm going to encourage the cows in this direction. All you have to do is point them into the pen." "All I have is this tennis racket," I said. "You have everything you need; trust me," he said as he drove away. Sure enough, the cattle came down the hill and I directed them into the pen with my Wilson tennis racket. I thought I was ill-equipped, but the rancher knew I had everything I needed.

When Moses was called to deliver God's people, he had a lot of excuses for why he wasn't the right guy for the job. At one point, Moses said to the Lord, "What if they do not believe me or listen to me?" Moses didn't think he was equipped to carry out this great deliverance ministry. And he was right. But God was going to do the equipping. I love what the Lord does next. He says to Moses, "What is that in your hand?" All Moses had was a staff. What could the Lord possibly do with a staff?

Then the Lord ordered Moses to throw the staff on the ground. You should read the story for yourself, but spoiler alert, it turned into a snake. Moses picked up the snake by the tail, because the Lord told him to, and it turned back into a staff. What was God trying to prove?

All the Lord needed from Moses was for him to give all that he had. God would do the rest. He would take what Moses had and empower him to deliver His people. All he had was a dirty, mangled staff. Fine. God can work with that. By the way, that staff would go on to part a sea, win battles and cause water to gush out of a rock.

So, what's in your hand? Will you give it to the Lord? It may not be much. It doesn't have to be much. God is not looking for you to become perfect before He uses you. He's just looking for you to say yes.

Every summer, my family travels to Minnesota to visit my wife's side of the family. On that side alone, my kids have 17 (and counting) cousins. One night my daughter Reese and her cousin Gwen were playing a board game. They didn't bother to read the directions, so they just made the rules up on their own. I was sitting nearby. Finally, they looked over at me and said, "This game is boring." To which I said, "It's only boring because you're playing it wrong."

I think a lot of people believe that the Christian life is boring. And I would say back, "It's only boring when you're playing it wrong."

Following Jesus should be the most exciting life you could ever live. It's a life of purpose. It's a life knowing and walking with the presence of God. It's a life where you get to be a part of bringing light into the darkness.

By the way, Elijah did leave his cave. He was reminded that God was with him. From there he lived out his purpose, which led to some great adventures. He parted the Jordan River with his cloak and was taken to Heaven in a whirlwind. That doesn't sound boring to me.

CHAPTER THREE

YOU ARE NOT ALONE

"The Lord Himself goes before you and will be with you; He will never leave you nor forsake you. Do not be afraid; do not be discouraged." **DEUTERONOMY 31:8**

Much of parenting is about helping a child become independent. You hold her hand when teaching her to walk, but hopefully not as she walks into her first day of high school. You teach him to look adults in the eye and respond respectfully and clearly. You take joy in the moments when your child does this on his own. But you have failed if you find yourself accompanying your 20-year-old in her job interview, reminding her to speak up and look the nice lady in the eye. We teach kids to look both ways before crossing the street so they will do it when we are not there. We want them to become independent. With God, however, the exact opposite is true. Our heavenly Father is not training us to be independent. Instead, He wants us to become completely dependent on Him.

Growing up in the Lord is about a growing dependence on Him. A mature follower of the Lord relies on Him through everything, counts on Him in everything, trusts Him with everything and pursues total dependence on Him. This kind of maturity is impossible if we don't say yes to the promise of God's presence. He is with us, and we grow in the Lord as we walk with Him. Much like you grow in any relationship, a thriving relationship with God happens as you speak with Him, listen to Him and follow Him. We praise God that He has promised to be with us. You are not alone, which is a good thing!

According to the Guinness Book of World Records, Hubert Wolfstern Sr. holds the record as the man with the longest name. Hubert had 26 first names — one for each letter in the alphabet. He also had a long last name. It was 666 letters long. Imagine trying to iron that onto the back of a basketball jersey. The only person who might have Hubert beat is Jesus. Our Lord was given many titles. He is called Almighty, Arm of the Lord, Author and Finisher of Our Faith, Beloved Son, Bread of Life, Cornerstone, Good Shepherd and Great High Priest, to name a few. But He was only given two first names, Jesus and Emmanuel.

The name Jesus means "the God who saves." This name honors Jesus for His power to deliver and rescue us from our sin. His name Emmanuel means "God is with us."

God is present.

Now.

With us.

I can't think of anything more profound, anything more important and anything more humbling than the fact that God is with us. When you experience God's presence, everything changes. This chapter is about God's promise to be with us. You are not alone. In fact, God's desire is for you to know the reality of His presence in your life more and more and become increasingly dependent on Him.

When my girls were young, they loved to play hide and seek. I would find the most difficult places to hide. They would search the whole house. I would hear them getting frustrated. When I detected that they were almost ready to give up, I would start whistling to help them find me. We should be thankful our heavenly Father doesn't play this way. He draws near to us as we draw near to Him (James 4:8). In Jeremiah 29:13, the Lord says, "You will seek me and find me when you seek me with all your heart." God is not hiding. He does not take joy in His children searching for Him without any luck. He promises to make Himself known as we turn to Him.

My youngest daughter Bria has been wearing glasses since she was in kindergarten. On most days, we spend several minutes trying to locate the misplaced glasses. Thankfully, I have always been able to find them because, without fail, they are in one of eight locations. All we do is go to the places where we know they can be found. Eventually, with enough patience and perseverance, they are found. The same principle can be applied when trying to find God. All we need to do is go to the places where we know He can be found.

Open His Word.

Spend time in prayer.

Welcome godly counsel.

Discover Him in His creation.

Serve the most vulnerable.

Step out in faith.

Go to the places where you know you can find Him.

THREE PROMISES ABOUT HIS PRESENCE

First, God is close. Let's turn back to the story of Elijah. In the book of 1 Kings Chapter 19, God called Elijah out onto a mountain. Elijah would have a front row seat to the presence of God passing in front of him. Scripture tells us that a great wind tore through the mountains. It was so strong the rocks shattered. But the Lord was not in the gusts of wind. Then there was an earthquake. But the Lord was not in the earthquake either. Then fire. But God was not in the fire. Finally, the Lord made Himself known to Elijah in the most unexpected way.

Through a whisper.

Why a whisper?

To hear someone whisper, you must be close. God revealed Himself through a whisper because He wanted to communicate an important truth to Elijah, "I am right here." This is still His message to us today. I used to think that God was up in Heaven looking down at us from a high place. But now I know that He is right here with us. I sense His presence as I meet with Him through prayer. He speaks to me as I listen with my heart. He is not throwing Hail Mary thunderbolts from Heaven. He is walking with us. He is close — close enough to whisper.

Second, God is moving. I was recently at a conference for a ministry that has a mission to strengthen and expand the church in the Middle East. Person after person came to the podium telling amazing stories about how God was doing even greater things than they could imagine. Over the course of three days, I heard incredibly powerful stories of God at work. One guy talked about their mission to smuggle Bibles into predominately Muslim areas. Carrying a Bible could get you arrested — or worse. Risking their own lives, they have published and handed out more than two million copies of the New Testament. Because of their boldness and commitment, many people are being impacted by the transforming message of Jesus. One woman shared about her opportunity to pray for her niece, who had a life-threatening disease. She was healed in front of her family and, as a result, they chose to follow Jesus as well. From stories of restored marriages, youth revivals, divine encounters and life-changing events, it was clear that God was on the move. And He still is.

The question is not whether God is moving; the question is, do we have the eyes to see Him? Are we connected to the activity of God? Are we looking? Are we ready to say yes to walking with Him?

There was a missionary in Africa who was "blessed" with someone's discarded automobile. The car would only start when it was in motion. So, the missionary figured out ways to get this treasure of a car moving before starting it. He would park on a hill or ask a group of people to give him a push before setting out. When he retired and a new missionary came to take his place, he was so excited to share about the car. He told him how to get the car started. The new missionary listened to him very closely. Then he opened the hood of the car, looked around a bit and asked for some tape. He quickly connected two wires that had come loose. He jumped into the car and started it right up – no hill or push necessary. The power was always available. There was just a loose connection.

This is how we often operate as Christians. The power is available, but the connection has not been made. God is always moving. The question is, are we connected? Saying YES to the promise of God's presence means eagerly welcoming the work of the Holy Spirit in our lives. This is how the connection is made. Through the filling of the Spirit, we are connected to the presence of God. Will you say yes to His presence? If so, this could be the most important thing you do today. Ask the Lord to fill you with His Spirit. Without the Spirit of God, we will miss out on the presence of God, the work of God and the power of God in our lives. We need the Spirit!

God is close, He is moving and, third, He can move through you. The Lord empowers His people to be His hands and feet. Throughout history, He has used His people to do His work. We can feel unworthy, but God wants to move through us. We so easily count ourselves out, thinking God must be looking for the best – but He is looking for those who will follow. He always advances the available. 2 Chronicles 16:9 says, "For the eyes of the Lord range throughout the earth to strengthen those whose hearts are fully committed to Him." God is looking for the committed. The presence of God is looking for people who will wholeheartedly commit to Him. And when He finds them, He moves through them.

It's so exciting when God works through us. It is such a joy to see the Lord move in power in and through His people. He is the one who makes our lives interesting. Without the Lord, Moses was just playing in the sea with a stick. But with God, he parted the waters and delivered the Israelites from bondage. Without the Lord, David was just a kid with a slingshot. But with God, he slayed the giant and became a mighty king. Without the Lord, Peter was just a fisherman. But with the Lord, he became the rock on which Jesus would build His church. Without the Lord, Mary was just a teenager. But with the Lord, she became the mother of the Son of God. Saying YES is so important because it's on the other side of YES that the presence of God moves through us. Where is God moving in your life? Will you say yes?

I was recently asked to give a blessing at a very formal event. The event was to raise funds for an animal sanctuary being built in honor of Catherine Violet Hubbard, one of the children who died in the Sandy Hook School shooting. The room would be filled with all kinds of people from many different religious backgrounds. I was asked by my friend Jenny, who is the founder of the sanctuary and Catherine's mom, to give a six-minute blessing. I was honored. But to be honest, totally nervous. I thought about what I was going to say and shared it with my wife. She told me I was playing it safe, which I was. She asked me if I had asked the Lord what He wanted me to say. I hadn't. I had just written a nice blessing – nothing more. Becca reminded me that I had been invited into this moment, and God wanted to do something through me.

After Becca's challenge, I turned to the Lord and asked Him what I should say. Almost immediately, the Lord spoke to my heart. I knew exactly what He wanted me to say; now I just had to say it. We arrived at the gala – I think that's what it's called. We pulled in behind a line of Range Rovers and Bentleys. Our silver minivan screeched as we came to a stop in front of the valet. We entered the event and I was invited to the podium. I stood before 500 guests and shared what the Lord placed on my heart. I shared about the prayer that Jesus taught His disciples to pray. In it, He teaches them to pray, "On earth as it is in Heaven." From this passage, I shared a blessing over the animal sanctuary that it would be a place where children and adults would experience Heaven on earth. In fact, I think it would be a great idea to place a sign over the main doorway that says, "Heaven on earth."

I sat down and felt a sense of peace about what I shared. An hour later, after the dinner had been served and the program continued, Jenny got up to the podium and introduced a video that had been prerecorded months earlier. The video was produced to communicate the vision of the sanctuary. I had never seen it before. Amazingly, in the video, Jenny shared that the vision for the sanctuary is that it would be "Heaven on earth." I was blown away. God had spoken to me. Much of the room turned around and pointed at me, as if to say, "You said that too. How did you know?" It was clear God showed up. It was such a powerful moment as God revealed Himself in real time. And I could have missed it had I not been reminded that God moves through us when we turn to Him.

God is on the move and doing greater things than we could ever imagine. This past Christmas Eve, I saw many people I hadn't seen in months. Several times these friends came up to me and asked, "Brian, what's new?" Each time I gave the stock answer, "Not much." On my way home, I found myself unsettled about my reply. Not much?

Really?

How untrue.

The answer should always be, "SO MUCH!" So much is going on. I vowed to never answer that question with, "Not much." In fact, if you're going to ask me that question, you better have a few hours on your hands. From smuggling Bibles to showing up at galas, God is on the move in powerful ways.

God is close. He is moving. And He is moving through us. So much is going on. But it all starts with us saying YES to His presence in our lives.

SECTION 2

SAY YES TO DEVOTION

"But for this purpose I have raised you up, to show you my power, so that my name may be proclaimed in all the earth." **EXODUS 9:16**

On the other side of our yes to the Lord is a deeper, more intimate relationship with Him and a greater ability to reflect His love to those we encounter each day. Ultimately, saying yes is about growing strong in our relationship with the Lord and serving our purpose of proclaiming His name throughout the earth. We praise God that He has committed to guiding us into an increasingly blessed life in Him. He has shown us the way, and He lights our steps. The pathway to a more intimate relationship with the Lord is through intentionality, commitment and devotion. Sadly, these are words in today's culture that are often avoided. Yet, the riches of a strong relationship with the Lord are not discovered through apathy but application. Not through unplanned coincidence but through the long-proven disciplines of the faith. This section is all about readopting the disciplines of the faith in a way that puts the emphasis on growing strong in our relationship with Jesus. These practical tools, called the disciplines of faith, are not to be used to judge or calculate the quality of our faith but instead to enhance and maximize the potential of our faith. These disciplines are things we do to grow strong in our relationship with the Lord. Practicing these disciplines is not faith. Instead, practicing these disciplines will strengthen your faith. The key verse in all this is 1 Timothy 4:7, "Discipline yourself for the purpose of godliness" (NASB). On the other side of your yes to His pathway is a rich relationship with Jesus.

CHAPTER FOUR
SAY YES TO PRAYER

"The Lord is near to all who call on Him." **PSALM 145:18A**

From the very first time I met Becca, I was enamored by her. Head over heels crazy about her. I remember we met at an Applebee's, where all timeless romances begin. A group of young adults would meet every Wednesday night for appetizers. On this occasion, Becca showed up and caught my attention right away. I now had another reason to attend the group besides the Jack Daniels Chicken. I remember she was wearing overalls with a white long sleeve shirt and her hair was done up in a ponytail. As I looked at her, I'm pretty sure time stood still. I will never forget that night.

Come to find out, she still doesn't remember meeting me.

But that was a small obstacle to overcome. This would not stop me from pursuing a life with her. From that moment, I determined that, whenever the group got together, I would strategically and I'm sure subtly secure one-on-one time with her. With it being October, a Christmas gift was in order. I got her what every girl wants — a compact disc (ancient way of playing music). Becca knew instantly that I was interested in her. I suspected my life was about to change.

It was the night of her office Christmas party. She called and asked if she could stop by my place after the party. There was something she wanted to tell me. I was so excited! I vacuumed the living room, wiped off the counters and even fluffed the one pillow on my futon. I imagined her coming in the door and announcing her love for me. The doorbell rang. I counted to five and then opened the door. She looked amazing. Decked out in leather pants and a beautiful red top, she was a showstopper. I on the other hand was wearing an old hoodie and jeans. She thanked me for the gift and then asked, "Can we just be friends?" Which really isn't a question.

I paused for a moment, picked up the shattered pieces of my heart and calmly stated, "I have enough friends."

I still don't know how I mustered the courage to say that, but she was shocked! I told her that I didn't want to hang out with her anymore because I wanted something much more than friendship.

We hugged.

She left.

And I'm pretty sure I cried.

When it comes to our relationship with Jesus, He is not looking to be added into our friend group. He's not asking, "Can we be friends?" Instead, He is inviting us to enter an intimate and personal walk with Him that will go deeper than any other relationship you could possibly imagine.

I want to challenge you to say yes to prayer. Prayer is God's chosen way for us to grow in our intimacy with Him. As we learn to speak with the Lord, we grow closer to Him. Much like any relationship, as we communicate with one another and share life together, our bond strengthens. Do you hunger for more of the Lord? Do you desire a deeper relationship with Him? Then you must say yes to prayer.

While Jesus was praying, one of the disciples approached Him and said, "Lord teach us to pray." This disciple had already seen Jesus heal and deliver people. He had already experienced the power of Jesus' name as he was sent out by Jesus Himself. Yet, when he saw Jesus praying, he saw that there was something more. Jesus had a unique connection with God. And this disciple wanted the same. He was a man of prayer. He knew how to pray well. But he wanted the kind of intimacy Jesus had with God. And he was bold enough to ask for it. The relationship Jesus had with God was different.

It was special.

It wasn't rehearsed.

It wasn't ritual.

It wasn't stale.

It was alive.

It was dynamic.

This chapter is about going deeper. It's about wanting more. It's about saying yes to prayer.

WHAT DOES IT MEAN TO SAY YES TO PRAYER?

Saying yes to prayer is saying yes to the revelation of God. Picture the lights at a concert. They can add so much to the show. The colors of the light provide mood, and the beams create eye-catching dimension. What you might not know is that, without a little haze (fog) in the room, you won't see the light beams. The light is already in the room, but you won't see the detail of the beams or the vibrancy of the colors. Prayer is the haze in the room. The presence of God is always there; however, when we pray, we release haze into the room, which allows us to see the detail of God's plans and the vibrancy of God's love. Prayer is not an obligation to do something; it's the opportunity to know someone.

When Jesus describes Himself as the good shepherd in John 10:27, He says, "My sheep listen to my voice." This implies that, when we know the good shepherd, we hear His voice. You might be wondering, "How do we hear the voice of God?" Praying is like learning to walk. You might wobble at first, but the more you practice the stronger you get. God speaks to us in many ways. I've experienced the Lord speaking to me through dreams, trusted friends, the circumstances of life and even through a simple thought that He places in my mind. Here are some suggestions that will help you learn to hear from God more clearly:

• Set time aside in your calendar.

• Find a quiet place where you can focus on the Lord.

• Ask the Lord what He wants to reveal to you.

• Open the Word of God. A great place to start is in the book of Psalms.

• Meet with friends who will help you discern what God is saying and doing in your life.

We often hear most clearly from the Lord while we are in motion. For me, I always hear from God best when I'm moving out in faith. In the middle of my step toward what I think God has called me to do and be, I hear God's voice more clearly. As a pastor, people come to me all the time asking why they haven't heard from God. They usually want to hear from God about what they should do with their life. Here's the thing. God has already told us what to do. God is waiting for you to get going on the things He has already told you to do:

• Love your neighbor.

• Forgive those who hurt you.

- Share Jesus with others.

- Feed the hungry.

- Meet the needs of the poor.

- Heal the sick.

- And the list goes on.

As you step out, more instructions from the Lord will follow. I'm confident you will hear from God while in motion.

Saying yes to prayer is saying yes to receiving the call of God. Through prayer, the Lord calls us to great things. There is a great story in Acts Chapter 10 about two men. One was named Peter and the other was named Cornelius. Both received a vision from the Lord that would change history. Peter was a Jew and Cornelius was a Gentile. Up to this point, the Gentiles were not considered a part of the people of God. But now the Lord was going to do a new thing. Peter was called by God to walk into Cornelius' house and welcome him into the family of God. In this moment, God was making it clear that the good news of Jesus was for all people. This moment changed history. And it all came from a vision from God. How did Peter and Cornelius receive this vision? What were they doing when they heard from God? Both were in prayer.

When you pray, expect God to respond. Be ready for the call of God. Your greatest assignments will be received through prayer.

Saying yes to prayer is saying yes to the power of God. Susan attended the church periodically. At the end of our church services, we always invite people to come forward for prayer. It is a blessing to pray for people in their season of hurt, trouble or celebration. One Sunday, Susan came forward for prayer. She asked me to pray for her because her right eye was constantly weeping. She had seen several doctors but was told nothing could be done. She was losing hope and was beginning to question whether God was with her in this struggle. I gathered a small group of my friends around her and we began to pray. I really sensed that the Lord wanted to do a special thing for her. We prayed that her eye would stop weeping and that she would know that God loved her. After several minutes of prayer, she looked up at us and her vision was completely restored. She started crying. Tears of joy streamed down her face because she was so moved by the power of God. He was there. He hadn't forgotten. Are you praying knowing that God has the power to cause breakthrough in your situation, in the difficulty you face and in the circumstances of your life? To pray is to believe that God is powerful. If we ask God for anything, we can believe that He has the power to accomplish it. When we approach the Lord in prayer, we are stepping into the presence of the almighty God, who can do immeasurably more than we could ever think or imagine.

Saying yes to prayer is saying yes to a way of life. Prayer is not an activity. It's a way of life. Activities begin and end, but with prayer, the Lord is calling us to be in constant communication with Him. Prayer is not a hobby. It's not like running or baking, where you can start and stop. Prayer should not be our last resort, but our first thought. Prayer is a relationship. It's a way of life, where we continually speak and listen to the Lord. When you say yes to prayer, you are not saying yes to an hour or a liturgy. You are saying yes to the second-by-second blessing of being in the presence of the Lord.

I love taking my kids mini golfing. Mainly because I can beat them. On one occasion, we were playing a hole where the obstacle was a giant octopus. Only one of the eight arms would lead to a hole in one. If you hit the ball into the correct arm of the octopus, the ball would go into the hole. I told the girls which arm to hit it into, but they kept missing. I explained the mystery of the octopus at least four times to the girls, without success. I finally stood over the correct arm and pointed at it saying, "Hit it here and it will go in." They continued to miss. It felt like they were getting worse. Finally, I figured out they were just messing with me. They were missing on purpose. I recorded every stroke in case you were wondering. When it comes to prayer, I picture the Lord saying to us, "This is the way to meet with me. This is the way to hear from me. Hit it here and it will go in."

HOW DOES GOD ANSWER OUR PRAYER?

As we say yes to prayer, we need to know how God answers prayer. God hears all our prayers, but He answers in different ways for different reasons. Sometimes He answers "yes." This is our favorite answer. There is very little complaining when God clearly says yes to our prayer. Sometimes He answers "No." This is when a door is clearly shut. Sometimes the Lord answers "wait." And sometimes we miss God's response entirely because we just don't like His answer.

WHY DOES GOD ANSWER "NO" OR "WAIT"?

Usually, the most difficult answers to receive from the Lord are no and wait. If we are going to be people who say yes to prayer, we need to understand why God might use these answers. I'm going to share eight reasons why God answers no or wait. Before I do, I want to be clear that there is not a one-size-fits-all answer to this question. Please don't apply all these answers to your situation. It could be that one of them applies. It could be that several of them apply. But not all will apply.

First, God might say no or wait because He has something far greater in mind. I remember saying no to Bria when she wanted an old cookie from home because I knew we were going to the ice cream store in just a few hours. Sometimes God says no or wait because He knows something far greater is ahead — far greater for you and, more importantly, far greater for His Kingdom.

Second, God might say no or wait because He wants to spare you from unseen harm. When Jimmy was six, he wanted fireworks for his birthday. He had a vision to put on the greatest fireworks show Upper 134th Street North had ever seen. Jimmy's dad did not share that same vision. Instead, his vision included driving Jimmy to the hospital to reattach his fingers. So, not surprisingly, Jimmy's dad said no. We must remember that God has a better view than we do. He knows what is best for us, and He often answers with a no because He wants to spare us from unseen harm. It could be that the heart throb you want to start a relationship with isn't as good as you think.

Or the company you want to work for is about to go through major layoffs. Maybe we should be thankful the door was shut.

Third, God might say no or wait because He has a better time. In real estate, it's about location, location, location. In our walk with the Lord, it's about timing, timing, timing. And the good news is that God has excellent timing. Sometimes God says no because He has a better time in mind.

One spring, my family decided to hatch chickens. We got eggs, put them in the incubator and waited. Every day Norah would come home and run to the incubator. To her it appeared like nothing was happening. They were just eggs. Day after day she came home hoping to see some sign of progress, only to be disappointed. Finally, Norah's patience had run out. She asked, "Can I just crack them open?" This would have been a bad idea. There was a lot going on under those shells. We just couldn't see it. Once they were fully developed, we celebrated as the chicks began to hatch. In our waiting, we can trust that God is working, and He has perfect timing.

Fourth, God might say no or wait because He wants to redirect you. The Apostle Paul wanted to go to Bithynia (Acts 16). The Spirit of the Lord would not allow Him to go and redirected him to a town where he met a woman named Lydia. She was a business leader with great influence in her community. Paul shared the good news of Jesus with her, and she and her whole family gave their lives to the Lord and were baptized. The Lord redirected Paul to do something far greater than he could have ever imagined.

Fifth, God might say no or wait because He is waiting for you to be obedient to Him. It might appear like we are waiting on God when He is waiting on us. God usually calls us to things step by step. We might be praying for a great opportunity, but God is waiting on us to take the first step toward that opportunity. Too often we are looking for shortcuts. Could it be that God has already given you the first step, and you just want to jump to the next one? Or could it be that God is asking you to step away from something and you haven't listened. Is there an unhealthy relationship, an addiction, a bad habit or an attitude God has asked you to leave behind? Maybe God wants you to be obedient to Him with what He has asked of you before opening the door to what you have asked of Him.

Sixth, God didn't say no; they did. Many people have persevered in prayer for others without seeing any change. What is happening? Doesn't God want them to kick their addiction? Wouldn't He be happy if they overcame their issue? Couldn't it bring Him great glory if they turned to Him? In this case, it's not God's no you are receiving; it's theirs. Maybe God has moved mountains to encounter the person you are praying for, yet he continues to refuse the Lord. With the ability to choose, he has chosen to go his own way. God doesn't force us to change. He has given us free choice, and we can use that free choice to turn to Him or away from Him.

Seventh, a battle was lost. This is probably the most difficult answer. We live in a world where the evil one is still at work. Until Jesus returns, the evil one will win some battles along the way. Friends are not healed. Loved ones don't return. Battles are lost.

Think of it this way. There has never been an NBA championship team that has won every game. They all suffered through losses leading up to the big game. Yet, they are still champions in the end. This is our story as well. In Jesus, we are victorious. Our championship day has not yet arrived. Until then, we will face losses along the way. But take hope in the fact that Jesus has overcome the world, and all will be put back to right upon His return.

Eighth, it could be that God hasn't answered because you haven't asked. Sometimes we get frustrated with the Lord over an unanswered prayer we have yet to pray. We may have wished for it, but never really prayed for it. Think of your current prayer request. Have you intentionally prayed? I ran through this list with one of my friends because he was wondering why the Lord hadn't answered his prayer. "That's it," he said. "I haven't really prayed for it."

WHERE DO I START?

Several years ago, our church launched an initiative we call the First 20. We challenged the whole church to spend the first 20 minutes of their day with Jesus. I often say your best 20 minutes. We have heard countless stories of people's lives being transformed through their First 20. Why? Because when you meet with Jesus, He changes your life. If we start our day with Jesus, there is a much better chance we will continue our day with Jesus. If you want to start a life of prayer, start first thing in the morning. In your First 20, read the Word of God, ask the Lord to empower you and invite the Lord to speak to you. And when He does, say yes.

And if you were wondering, after Becca rejected me, two days later she called me back and asked me out to dinner. On the other side of her no, she said yes.

CHAPTER FIVE

SAY YES TO FASTING

"Is not this the kind of fasting I have chosen: to loose the chains of injustice and untie the cords of the yoke, to set the oppressed free and break every yoke?" **ISAIAH 58:6**

My 16th birthday was not all I hoped it would be. It was memorable, but memorable does not always mean good. I was on an outdoor adventure trip with my church youth group in the Adirondack Mountains in Upstate New York. The trip was designed to challenge students in their faith and equip them to be leaders. We hiked to the top of several mountains, learned how to rock climb, conquered a high ropes course and ran a 10-mile race to culminate the adventure. One of the challenges was particularly difficult for me, and it happened to land on my 16th birthday. The leaders, who we were told to call Sherpas, walked each of us to separate parts of the woods. I'm not sure why we trusted these Sherpas. They were just college kids in need of some cash. Experienced Sherpas don't cry every night before bed because they miss their girlfriends. The Sherpas left us each on our own for two days with nothing but a sleeping bag, Bible, water bottle and tarp. Turns out I would need the tarp because it rained for 40 of the 48 hours. The challenge was to meet the Lord through solitude and fasting. The evening of the first day, the "Sherpas" visited me because it was my birthday. They brought a cupcake with a candle in it. They lit the candle, sang happy birthday, took the cupcake with them and left me to be alone again. Thanks a lot!

My fasting experience did not start out well. It was like a bad blind date who I knew nothing about. My Sherpa friends left me to figure it all out on my own. What has been your experience with fasting? When Jesus speaks about fasting in Matthew's Gospel, He talks about when we fast. He never says if you fast. There is this assumption that we will fast. I think fasting can be confused as something only the super spiritual do; however, Jesus assumes all who follow Him will fast. I'm not writing this chapter as a fasting master but as a learner. So, let's say yes together.

There is a moment in the Gospel of Matthew when Jesus is asked why His disciples don't fast. While Jesus walked with them on earth, they did not fast. Jesus answers by saying, "The time will come when the bridegroom will be taken from them; then they will fast" (Matthew 9:15). Fasting was associated with mourning and was usually a sign of brokenheartedness. It was a sign of a person's desperation for something. The Jewish people would fast because they were desperate for the Messiah to come – the bridegroom – the promised One God would send to redeem the world through a new covenant. The disciples did not fast because the bridegroom was with them. There was

CHAPTER FIVE: SAY YES TO FASTING 57

no need to fast; it was party time. After a thousand years of waiting and hoping for the Messiah to come, He was now here. Therefore, fasting was not for them. Fasting was for when the bridegroom left.

Jesus says, "Then they will fast." When? He was pointing to the days between His resurrection and return. That means the time for fasting is now.

We know that Jesus is present with us now through His Holy Spirit, but Paul says in 2 Corinthians 5:8 that we would "prefer to be away from the body and at home with the Lord." In other words, there is an ache, a longing and a homesickness within every follower of Jesus because He is not here as intimately and fully as we want Him to be. We take joy in the fact that we have a down payment of His presence through the gift of His Spirit, but we long for the full measure of His presence that is promised upon His return. We fast until that day when Jesus returns to bring us home.

Fasting is possibly the most forgotten, misunderstood and sadly avoided gift that God has given us. This hidden gift will only be enjoyed when we better understand its purpose and experience its blessings.

WHAT IS FASTING?

Biblical fasting is about abstaining from food for spiritual enrichment. The normal practice for fasting was abstaining from solid foods for a set period of time to intentionally concentrate on focused prayer.

Yet, as we will talk about later, a fast does not have to be limited to solid foods. It might not be healthy for you to fast from solid foods. We can fast from technology, social media or certain foods. These types of fasts can be equally fulfilling.

Fasting was a normal part of the Jewish culture in the first century. People would fast twice a week. The Day of Atonement was also a national day of fasting. On this day, people would make a sacrifice to the Lord for their sins. The early church also fasted twice a week, usually on Monday and Friday. This practice was carried out through the fourth century. During Easter, Christians would fast for 40 days. Baptism candidates would fast for 40 days leading up to their baptism. Imagine being told you had to fast for 40 days before being baptized. Would we have anyone wanting to be baptized? Church leaders such as Charles Finney, Charles Spurgeon, Jonathan Edwards, Martin Luther, John Calvin, D.L. Moody and John Wesley personally fasted and made it a requirement for all ordained ministers to fast twice a week.

WHY IS FASTING IMPORTANT?

Most of the reasons fasting is important are spiritual in nature; however, fasting is also good for a person's health. According to Healthline Research, there are several scientifically proven benefits to fasting, including blood sugar control, the decrease of inflammation, improved blood pressure, a boost in brain function, increased metabolism and greater levels of human growth hormones.

FIVE SPIRITUAL BENEFITS OF FASTING

To Reprioritize

God calls us to fast on purpose. Through fasting, we reorder our lives and put things in the right place. If things in our lives are not prioritized correctly, we get out of alignment and everything we do suffers. Imagine a ship that is off course by just a few degrees. The farther it travels, the more distant it will become from its hoped-for destination. Fasting resets our spiritual lives and reorders our priorities.

As humans, we are composed of body, soul and spirit. In his letter to the church in Thessalonica, the Apostle Paul says, "May God Himself, the God of peace, sanctify you through and through. May your whole spirit, soul and body be kept blameless at the coming of our Lord Jesus Christ" (1 Thessalonians 5:23).

Our body is the physical shell that allows us to interact with the world. We see and hear. We touch, taste and smell.

Our soul is our mind, emotion and will. Our mind enables us to do things like think, reason, consider, remember and wonder. Our emotions allow us to have feelings like happiness, sorrow, anger, relief and compassion. And our will enables us to make decisions to move forward through life. Our soul is our personality.

Our Spirit is the core of our being and is even deeper than the soul. Through our Spirit, we can connect with God. Through our Spirit, we can know God.

Now this is the important part!

In God's design, the perfect order goes like this. The Lord comes first. He is to be given rule and reign in our lives. The Lord is to take priority over everything else. From here, the Lord governs and speaks to the Spirit within us. This is the Spirit of Christ Jesus. The Spirit then tells our soul who we are and how we are to think. Through the Spirit, our soul finds its identity. We are children of God. Then our bodies follow the soul. The body takes its marching orders from what we think and feel. After this, we are placed in the world. We are called to take our bodies and bring the light of Jesus into our world. This is God's perfect design for us.

Lord – **Spirit** – Soul – Body – World

But there is a problem. This isn't how it always works. Sadly, we are easily distracted and can flip His perfect design upside down.

We prioritize the things of the world. The world dictates what we do and how we act. Other people (such as politicians, movie stars and rock stars) influence who we are and what we think. From here, our bodies act in the way the world wants them to. This affects our soul. Our identities are found based on the affirmation we receive from the world. Our personalities reflect the latest fads and opinions of the world. This usually results in ignoring the Spirit. And, tragically, the

Lord is left out altogether.

World — Body — Soul — (Spirit) — Lord

We must remember the battle we are fighting. We are fighting against God's adversary, the evil one. And he is at work flipping God's design upside down. Instead of being defined by the inside out, we are being defined from the outside in.

The way to break this bondage is to decree it is not going to be so. When you fast, you are taking the pattern of the world and reordering it correctly. Through fasting, we put the Lord where He belongs. How do you do this? You start with the world and what it offers — food, technology, social media. And then you move to the body. You tell your body what is going to happen. I am going to deprive you of food.

Beware, the body will throw a temper tantrum. "I need chocolate!!!"

Then you intentionally focus on the Lord. There is spiritual significance in this action. You are declaring allegiance to the Lord while neglecting the body what it desires. You are making a decree. The Lord is on top. The Lord is most important in my life. I can resist the things of this world, but I can't live without the Lord.

The benefits are significant. The Lord is placed in His rightful place. Our identities are secured as children of God. We experience a closeness with the Lord. And, as we experience the closeness of the presence of God, He speaks to us. Saying yes to fasting is not easy, but necessary as we live in this world awaiting His promised return.

To Worship

Fasting is also an act of worship to the Lord, because you are sacrificing lower goods for greater goods. It becomes a sacrifice of praise to the Lord. When we fast, we are declaring that God is more important than anything else.

I drive a Ford truck. I love trucks. But that really has nothing to do with this story, besides the fact that my daughter Norah and I were in the truck when this story happened. Sometimes I let my kids play on a phone while we are driving. I gave my phone to Norah when we got in the truck. We made our way to wherever we were going. Five minutes into the drive, I looked in the rearview mirror and saw Norah put the phone down. She looked up and said, "Papa, how's your day going?" I almost started crying. Isn't this what every parent wants — to win the attention of our kids over the game Minesweeper (or whatever game they are playing back there). My heart was warmed when Norah chose me over the thing of this world. She asked me all kinds of questions. I was able to answer a few of them. It was beautiful. But it would have never happened if she didn't put the phone down.

Fasting is when we put down the phone. The food. The remote.

When we fast, we sacrifice something to be attentive to God. It's saying, "Lord, I'm going to give up on food today. When my stomach groans, I'm going to look to you. I'm going to turn my attention and affection to you."

To Fellowship

Fasting clears the way to grow in our fellowship with God. The early church in Acts Chapters 13-14 gathered to pray and fast. They did this to ask God for direction. They wanted to know where to go and what to do. So, they cleared the way for God to speak to them through prayer and fasting. You can't overstate the importance of this moment in the life of the church. The Spirit guided the church in this moment. Through prayer and fasting, the church heard from the Lord. The result changed history.

After this decision to pray and fast, Paul and Barnabas were sent out. Paul made his missionary journeys. He wrote the letters we read in the Bible today. Christianity was spread throughout the world after the church stopped to pray and fast. From this moment in history, we learn that fasting allows us to hear and see more profoundly the things of God. It clears the static and brings us into greater fellowship with the Lord.

To Bless Others

This might surprise you, but fasting stirs our hearts for others. It positions us to bless others. Fasting is the avenue to discern the heart of God. When this happens, we gain the heart of God for others. In Isaiah 58, the prophet says, "Is not this the kind of fasting I have chosen: to loose the chains of injustice and untie the cords of the yoke, to set the oppressed free and break every yoke?" In this passage, we learn where fasting should lead us. True fasting is about learning how to bless God and others. God truly loves His people; therefore, we should not be surprised that, through prayer and fasting, He draws our hearts to those He loves.

To Intensify the Power of Prayer

Prayer is always a part of fasting. They go together like peanut butter and jelly — unless you are allergic to peanuts. Then this doesn't work for you. How about milk and cookies? Nonetheless, fasting intensifies the power of prayer.

In the book of Nehemiah, we learn that he prayed and fasted for his city that laid in ruins. He wanted to return to his city to rebuild the walls. Through prayer and fasting, the Lord responded to Nehemiah. There is power in prayer and fasting. When we remove the static and get in step with the Spirit of God, we put ourselves in the right position to hear from God and do powerful things for Him. If we want to see God move in radical ways, we must be willing to do radical things. We cannot manipulate God to do anything; however, as His children, we can certainly come into His presence boldly. Biblically, we see that prayer and fasting are a powerful combination. Continually, when God's people prayed and fasted, the Lord moved in power.

For what are you praying and fasting? Or for what will you pray and fast? Do you have friends who need to meet Jesus? Do you have a son or daughter who is wandering? Are there areas in your life in which you desperately need God to move? Are you wondering where to go or what to do? Is it time for you to say yes to fasting?

HOW SHOULD WE FAST?

In Matthew Chapter 6, Jesus teaches us how to fast. We are told not to make a spectacle of it. Fasting is not done to look good. If you are fasting for the approval of others, that is the only reward you will get. Some people might think you are very spiritual. Instead, our motivation should be to meet with God, hear His voice, know His heart and boldly bring our requests before Him. With this attitude, we will be amazed at the blessings we receive as we pray and fast.

As you enter a fast, I would encourage you to do these four things. 1) Pray. Ask the Lord when and how long you should fast. Pray about whether you should fast from solid food or something else. 2) Have an objective. It may be to grow closer to the Lord, which is a worthy objective; however, is there another reason as well? Having an objective will help you focus on how to pray. 3) Prepare for your fast. Plan out your fast. Schedule it. When will you pray? What will you be praying for? Who will join you in your fast? Prepare spiritually as well as practically. Ask the Lord to protect your fast. Invite a few others to pray for you during your fast. 4) As you begin fasting, make sure to enter and exit slowly. Wean yourself on and off solid foods. Start with a one-day fast before ever considering a 10-day fast or a 40-day fast.

Saying yes to fasting should be done with intentionality. Don't just follow any "Sherpa" out into the woods for a fasting experience. Instead, say yes to fasting with purpose. Start by choosing a day or two days. Write down a list of three to five things you are going to specifically pray about. As you are fasting and praying, write down the things that God reveals to you. Enjoy His presence.

CHAPTER SIX

SAY YES TO FORGIVENESS

"Bear with each other and forgive one another if any of you has a grievance against someone. Forgive as the Lord forgave you." **COLOSSIANS 3:13**

When I was a kid, the Big Wheel was the greatest toy on the planet. And I had a rad Big Wheel. The handlebars were yellow, and the royal blue seat rested on a bright red chassis. The wheels were made from "indestructible" plastic, and the adventure began when the "Big Wheel" inevitably dented. But that did not stop me from flying down my parents' steep driveway, feet off the pedals, wind in my hair, without a care in the world. Those were some of the best days — until my brother ruined everything. Somehow, he convinced me he could transform my sick ride into a gas-powered go-kart. I'm not sure why I believed him. I had never seen him work on anything mechanical. Would his Lego building translate? In the end, my Big Wheel was left in pieces and I'm still waiting for that promised go-kart.

I've since forgiven my brother. If you didn't know that already, Craig,

I forgive you, unless you haven't made it this far in the book, then I might reconsider. I'm sure you have been hurt much worse than I was with my Big Wheel. All of us have been the victims of other people's poor choices. In one sense, we all need each other so much, yet we cause each other great pain. People hurt people. Saying yes to forgiveness is not easy. How should we respond when words are used against us? What are we to do when a person harms us? Where should we turn when we're abandoned?

God knows what's best for us. This is why He calls us to forgive. When we say yes to forgiveness, we say yes to our healing and restoration.

WHAT IS FORGIVENESS?

To forgive means to release or send away. This is so hard for us to do. Our natural desire is to hold on to the grudge and to keep wrongs and offenses close. We like to say things like, "Let's bury the hatchet," which means leaving the issue behind and moving forward. The problem is, after we "bury the hatchet," we usually carry with us a detailed map to where we buried the hatchet so we can dig it up whenever we need to wave it in our offender's face. Listen, it's alright to keep a picture of the hatchet. You will always remember what it looks like and even what it felt like, but forgiveness means getting rid of the map. When we get rid of the map, we release and send away the offense.

I think we need a gutsier definition for forgiveness. To release and send away is good, but I don't think it portrays biblical forgiveness well enough. Thomas Watson was a pastor, preacher and author in the late 1600s. He defined forgiveness this way, "When we strive against all thoughts of revenge; when we will not do our enemies harm, but wish well to them, grieve at their calamities, pray for them, seek reconciliation with them, and show ourselves ready on all occasions to relieve them." This is biblical forgiveness.

It's a high calling.

It's a difficult calling.

It's the way of Jesus.

Forgiveness is not forgetting.
To forgive and forget is an impossibility. When we are hurt, we can't just forget that hurt and wipe it from our minds. We don't have that kind of superpower. Praise God if He chooses to take those memories from you, but don't expect forgiveness to wipe the memories away completely.

I still remember the Big Wheel.

Forgiving someone means that every time the wrong comes to mind, we forgive again. You might feel like you have failed in forgiving because you haven't forgotten the offense. If you remember the offense, that does not mean you have failed to forgive. The questions become, "Will you forgive again? Will the offense be a picture, or will you go and dig it up again? Will you allow it to control your life, or will you release it?"

Forgiveness is not restored trust.

When you forgive, it doesn't mean you must fully trust the person who hurt you. Forgiveness is chosen, and trust is earned. It's probably not a good idea to leave your wallet out in front of the person who stole from you. It's natural to question the whereabouts of a spouse who has betrayed you.

Jim and Dana had been married for 15 years. Sadly, Jim started a relationship with another woman. After a strong feeling of conviction, Jim confessed to his wife and ended the other relationship. Amazingly, Dana forgave him. I met with the couple several times through this difficult season. I remember one session when Jim came in very upset. Dana kept asking to see his phone. Jim said, "I thought she forgave me. Why does she need to see my phone?" I told him, "You have her forgiveness. Now earn her trust." It was time for some tough love. I told Jim he needed to do everything he could to regain her trust.

Share the passwords.

Share the calendar.

Let her see the browser history.

Invite her to look at the phone.

Give her access to your email.

View your social media together.

Get an accountability partner.

Do everything you can to earn her trust.

Forgiveness does not mean trust automatically and effortlessly returns. Instead, forgiving allows the opportunity for trust to be restored.

Forgiveness does not mean minimizing the offense.

Offenses should be taken seriously. The consequences and effects of the wrongs committed should not be passed off as inconsequential or insignificant. We often withhold our forgiveness because we think that it will let our offender off the hook and, even worse, communicate that the offense wasn't that bad. We think that somehow forgiving is admitting the wrong was not very wrong after all, or the hurt was not painful. The truth is forgiveness does not minimize the offense or deny that you're still hurting. It maximizes the chance for peace in our lives. Forgiveness has very little to do with the offense and very much to do with our own well-being. Forgiveness is not the eraser; it's the ink. Through forgiveness, we don't wipe away the past. We begin to write a new chapter. The last chapter is not forgotten, but a new chapter is now possible.

Forgiveness is a choice, and restoration is the process.

When I first began to drive, I avoided the highway and was especially nervous to merge into traffic. For months, I would only travel on the back roads dodging deer, hitting potholes, avoiding those annoying fall leaf peepers and burning more gasoline than my $8 an hour job could support. Avoidance was becoming costly and there were places the backroads could not take me. I eventually had to get on the highway. Too often, I hear people considering forgiveness. I know forgiveness is hard, but it's the only road that leads us to restoration.

Forgiveness is not easy.

It's not easy to ask for forgiveness, and it's not easy to forgive. When we look through our human lenses, we see all the difficulties to forgiveness. Do I really need to ask for forgiveness? Wouldn't I be letting them off the hook if I forgive? They hurt me so badly, how can I possibly forgive? The good news is that God anoints us for the tough things in life. When we embrace this call, He anoints us with a special ability to forgive.

THE DANGERS OF UNFORGIVENESS

When we refuse to forgive, we refuse the good things God provides on the other side of forgiveness.

Unforgiveness hurts our identity.

When I was a kid, I had a bad temper. The littlest of things could set me off. My emotions were completely determined by outside influences. If one of my siblings said something I didn't like, I would snap. If the weather kept me from going outside, I would mope around the house. If a friend were mean to me, I would fight back. Outside influences played my emotions like a fiddle, determined my outlook on life and began to define my identity. I was becoming known as the kid who always lost his temper.

In Luke 6:27-31, Jesus teaches the disciples about loving their enemies by saying, "Do good to those who hate you. Bless those who curse you. Pray for those who hurt you." This may not have been what they wanted to hear, but Jesus was teaching them two important principles. The first was the principle of love. His disciples were to love with an extravagant love. The second was the principle of protection. Jesus wanted them to protect their status as children of God. Outside influences were not to define them. In the face of offense, Jesus was calling them to stay rooted in the Lord.

Jesus modeled this in His own life. His identity wasn't lost because Judas betrayed Him. He didn't lash out when Peter denied Him. He didn't compromise His character when people spat on Him and crucified Him. He didn't allow offenses to define Him. His identity never bowed to outside influences. When we refuse to forgive, we allow the offense to become our identity. It clings to us and we become the kid who always lost his temper. Too many of us have surrendered to a false identity that has now defined us.

We have become the person who was overlooked.

The person who was offended.

The person who was abandoned.

The person who was betrayed.

But when we forgive, we make a declaration over the offense. We tell the offense it won't define us, and we secure our identity in the Lord.

Offenses are guaranteed. In fact, I once heard Pastor T.D. Jakes say, "If you're going to do great things in the Kingdom of God, you're going to meet great offenses. New levels bring new devils." Expect offenses. You will receive them, but you don't have to keep them. God gives us great wisdom in Proverbs 17:9 when He tells us, "Whoever would foster love covers over offense." This is why we need Jesus. His love covers over every offense.

Unforgiveness hurts our bodies.

In a John Hopkins Medicine article entitled "Forgiveness: Your Health Depends on It," unforgiveness was linked to cardiovascular disease, hypertension, high blood pressure and cancer. In a study called "Forgive to Live," Luther College psychologist Loren Toussaint discovered there are health benefits to being able to practice unconditional forgiveness. There is a difference between conditional and unconditional forgiveness. When a person practices conditional forgiveness, he forgives based on a set of predetermined criteria. If the person asks for forgiveness, he will be forgiven. Or if the person shows the kind of remorse that we would like, then he will be forgiven. Only when these conditions are met will forgiveness be granted. Toussaint discovered that people who practice conditional forgiveness have sets of rules that make forgiveness impossible. Instead, they hold on to the hurt, stress levels rise, and their health begins to deteriorate.

On the other hand, for those who practice unconditional forgiveness, the health benefits are great. Through his research, Toussaint found that people who can forgive without special requirements end up living longer. In an article by Psychology Today entitled "Live

Longer by Practicing Forgiveness," the author commented on one of Toussaint's findings, "If you decide to forgive the wrongdoer without an apology, then you can start the process at any time. The sooner the psychological healing begins, the more likely it is that your health will reap the benefits." Receiving an apology may not happen, but we can still forgive and reap the benefits in our personal lives. If you want to hold out for that Hollywood moment when the one who hurt you shows up in the rain and pleads for your forgiveness in front of all your neighbors, all you are doing is delaying freedom and restoration in your own life. The gift of forgiveness is for you. On the other side of your choice to forgive is a healthier and more fulfilling life.

Unforgiveness hurts our fellowship.

Steve and Julie had been married for 10 years when Steve made a risky financial investment without consulting Julie. Hoping things would turn around, Steve kept it from Julie as long as he could. But things were not getting better. Within five months, all their savings had been depleted. It came time for Steve to fess up. As you can imagine, Julie was not happy. Two years had passed when they met with me to discuss their issue. At this point, Steve had apologized hundreds of times. He began sitting with Julie every Monday night to go over their finances. He was doing everything he could to gain back her trust. I asked Julie, "What is keeping you from forgiving him?" Without hesitation, she looked at me and said, "He can't get away with this." Unfortunately, their marriage was going down the tubes. Steve was constantly anxious around Julie, and Julie was continually upset with Steve. I calmly looked back at Julie and said, "The only one getting away with anything right now is the one who wants your marriage to fall apart. Unforgiveness has given the evil one a foothold into your relationship, and it's being torn apart. Steve isn't getting away with anything, but if you're not careful, the evil one will come and take everything."

When we refuse to forgive, we are refusing restored relationship. Julie had to forgive if she wanted to see her marriage thrive. That doesn't mean the restoration process would be easy – but it would mean the chance for a healthy and fulfilling life together. The same is true in our friendships and in our family life. If the marriage is going to thrive, forgiveness must be a key ingredient. If the friendship is going to grow, forgiveness and grace must be at the center. If the church is going to reflect the love of Jesus, forgiveness must be learned and practiced.

Unforgiveness hurts our usefulness.

When I was a freshman in college, I was on the hockey team. It was very rare that a freshman would get any game time. Our role was to ride the bus and give our full support – no equipment necessary. Call me a hopeless optimist, but I always brought my gear in case of an unlikely miracle or a Tanya Harding reenactment. Turns out, just before the game, one of our starters was rushed off to the ER to pass a kidney stone. The coach needed a substitute. He looked around the room in mild desperation. Who would step into the third line winger position? Who could fulfill this heavy burden on such short notice? Frankly, and more accurately, who had skates? This guy. I played my first college hockey game as a freshman all because I was ready to be called in. 2 Chronicles 16:9 says, "For the eyes of the Lord range throughout the earth to strengthen those whose hearts are fully committed to him." God is always looking for those whose hearts are fully surrendered to Him. He is looking for those who are ready to step in. Ready to serve. Ready to be used for His glory. When we choose to forgive, we put ourselves in a position to be used powerfully by God.

SAY YES TO FORGIVENESS

I'm reminded of Joseph in the Bible. He was sold into slavery by his own brothers, but he remained faithful to the Lord. Over time, Joseph found himself as the chief advisor to Pharaoh in Egypt. A famine struck the land and Joseph's brothers were sent to Egypt to get food. Their younger brother, who they sold into slavery, was the guy who had the power to provide for their needs. Imagine being Joseph. Your brothers are standing in front of you, but they don't recognize you. You are now their only hope. How would you respond?

"Off with their heads."

"Kiss my feet."

"Replace my Big Wheel."

Joseph takes a different approach. He forgives them. And in the end, he abundantly blesses them. How we respond matters to the Lord. I'm sure it wasn't the easiest thing for Joseph to forgive his brothers, but it was the best thing. Through forgiveness, his family was restored. Do you need to say yes to forgiveness? On the other side of your choice to forgive, God is ready to meet you with grace and love and walk with you as a new chapter is written.

CHAPTER SEVEN

SAY YES TO PEACEMAKING

"Blessed are the peacemakers, for they will be called children of God." **MATTHEW 5:9**

I grew up in a neighborhood full of kids riding bikes and playing sports. Street hockey was one of our favorites. We were playing one day, and I was the target, otherwise known as the goalie ... again. Wearing inadequate padding, I stood in the net as my older brother wound up like Al Iafrate on a breakaway. I'm certain my Franklin baseball mitt was not manufactured to withstand this kind of heat. According to the NHL rule book, the main objective is to try and shoot the puck into the net, but my brother formulated a new game called, "How many times can I hit Brian where he has no padding?" Or, equally as fun, "How many slap shots will it take to make Brian bleed?" I never responded well. Somewhere between 10 and 12 direct hits, the driveway became a yard sale of sports equipment as I threw sticks, gloves and often the entire net at my brother.

As we journey through life, we will get hit. Sometimes it will even feel like the world is targeting the spots in our life that are most vulnerable.

Our hard work will go unnoticed.

Our plans will be frustrated.

Our good deeds will be taken advantage of.

Our loved ones will be treated unfairly.

Our integrity will be challenged.

Jesus tells us very specifically, "In this world you will have trouble" (John 16:33). This is not the kind of guarantee we like to embrace. We live in a world that is far from peaceful. The horrors of slavery continue as our most defenseless are targeted and treated inhumanely. War and conflict are a normal part of our daily news feeds. Relationships are breaking up all around us. Differing opinions on topics such as politics, religion and even sports stir up unhealthy hostility among us. In today's world, conflict is not difficult to find.

CARRY PEACE

Jesus taught His disciples how to live in a hostile world. He taught them to carry peace. To be a disciple means to follow the example of Jesus. When He sent out 72 of His disciples, He gave them very clear instructions. They were not to pack any extras.

No spending cash.

No spare socks.

No snacks.

Right after these instructions, Jesus tells them what they were to carry. It was not anything they could hold in their hands. It could only be carried in their hearts and shared through their words. They were to carry peace. Upon arriving in someone's home, Jesus instructed them to say, "Peace to this house" (Luke 10:5).

Jesus was called the Prince of Peace (Isaiah 9:6). On the day of His birth, the angels sang, "Glory to God in the highest Heaven, and on earth peace to those on whom His favor rests" (Luke 2:14). When a woman touched the edge of Jesus' robe and was healed, He said to her, "Go in peace" (Luke 8:48). Before His death, Jesus said to His disciples, "Peace I leave with you; my peace I give you" (John 14:27). And after His resurrection, He appeared before His disciples saying, "Peace be with you" (Luke 24:36). To follow Jesus means to carry peace.

Not hatred.

Not envy.

Not jealousy.

Not selfishness.

Not anger.

Not pride.

But peace!

During one of Jesus' sermons, He told the crowd, "Blessed are the peacemakers, for they will be called children of God" (Matthew 5:9). Part of what makes us the children of God is that we are peacemakers. Becca and I have been teaching our kids to look out for other kids who might need a friend. After months of extensive training, I saw one of my daughters go up to a kid at the bus stop who was all alone. She invited her to play with the rest of the group. In my head I remember thinking, "That's my girl!" She had done what she had been taught and it filled me with joy. When we live out our call to be peacemakers, I believe the Lord says, "That's my girl!" "That's my boy!" Proudly, He delights in us as we step into our calling to bring peace. Are you carrying peace?

In your home?

In your workplace?

In your relationships?

In your heart?

What is peace?

For many, peace is believed to be the absence of conflict. Under this belief, a person will tend to avoid conflict and confrontation at all costs, believing such circumstances could not coexist with peace. This leads to counterfeit peace. It is not real peace; it is the appearance of peace. With this kind of peace, we keep silent when a friend is heading down a dangerous path because speaking up could rock the boat. Or even worse, we allow unhealthy things to exist in our relationships to avoid conflict. Truth goes unspoken in favor of the absence of confrontation.

But this is not peace.

The word peace in the Greek language is "eirene." In its fullness, this word encompasses three areas of health and wholeness:

- Inner health and wholeness — the tranquil state of the soul

- Right relationships with one another — a peace that brings harmony among individuals, groups of people and nations

- Right relationship with God

The Hebrew word is "shalom," which means complete peace. Therefore, peace is an inner sense of contentment and confidence because of a right relationship with God that encourages right relationships with one another.

The question becomes, "How do we achieve this kind of peace?" The 2019 Global Peace Index outlines the eight pillars of positive peace. These are the eight things, if present, that will lead to peace:

1. Well-Functioning Government

2. Equitable Distribution of Resources

3. Free Flow of Information

4. Good Relations with Neighbors
   (I think they stole this from the Bible.)

5. High Levels of Human Capital

6. Acceptance of Rights of Others

7. Low Levels of Corruption

8. Sound Business Environment

The eight pillars of positive peace provide us with a well-thought-out plan, but it's missing the most critical aspect of peace: the source — Jesus.

Shalom, complete peace, is only realized through the Prince of Peace. Because of the work of Jesus, we can have a right relationship with God. Through obeying Jesus, His teachings and the promptings of His Spirit, we can live in healthy relationships with one another. And because of the gift of the Holy Spirit in our lives, we can experience inner peace. The eight pillars are not enough. It doesn't matter how well we practice the eight pillars. If we don't have the one pillar who brings peace, all is for naught. There is one pillar who leads us to complete peace, and His name is Jesus. Peace is not something you can manufacture on your own. It is a gift from God. It is a divine work. God alone is the author of peace. Therefore, peace is not the absence of something. It is the presence of our great comforter.

PEACE KRYPTONITE

My high school hockey team had a rival. The games we played against them were always hard-fought battles. I can still remember my senior year when we played the Hawks in the championship game of our conference. We knew if we were going to win, we had to find a way to shut down their star player Tyler. We came up with what we called the Kryptonite Plan. My friend Eric was assigned to skate right next to Tyler and harass him the whole game. We ended up winning because we took Tyler off his game. He became agitated and was distracted from his purpose.

This is the same strategy implemented by the evil one to throw us off course and shut down our effectiveness for the Lord. Our kryptonite is fear. When we are gripped with fear, peace is lost. 1 Peter 5:7 says, "Cast all your anxiety on Him because He cares for you." If we want to be people who carry peace, we need to cast our fear and anxiety away. So how is this done?

First, we need to replace worry with the Word. God's Word is a gift to us. When we meditate on the good news of Jesus, our fears and anxieties are drowned out by God's great love for us. Concentrate on the promises of God instead of the "what-ifs" of life. Focus on the truth instead of the "could-ofs" we hear in the news. When we replace worry with the Word, we move from a position of being sent wherever the wind blows to a strong foundation in the Lord. Samantha has always struggled with worry and anxiety. When she heard this teaching, she decided to post Scripture verses on her bathroom mirror so that she would see them first thing in the morning. Before she is ever able to start down the path of worry, her mind is focused on the promises of God. Maybe it would be a good idea for you to try this. I'll give you a great one to start with, "The Lord is near. Do not be anxious about anything, but in every situation, by prayer and petition, with thanksgiving, present your requests to God. And the peace of God, which transcends all understanding, will guard your hearts and your minds in Christ Jesus" (Philippians 4:5-7).

Second, we need to share our worry with others. A life following Jesus is not always easy. We are called to the tough stuff. I cannot imagine taking this journey of faith alone. We all need a crew of people in our lives who we can speak with, pray with and walk with. No fear should be faced alone. Rely on the blessing of others to help you overcome your fears. For some who particularly struggle with fear and anxiety, you will need to regularly meet with a Christian counselor. God often uses the wisdom and coaching of others to help us through seasons we cannot manage on our own.

Third, we need to stop worry early. Worry acts like a snowball racing down a mountain. The more time we allow it to roll down the hill, the bigger it becomes. When we sense fear and anxiety creeping up, we need to address it early. The best way to grocery shop is with a list. You shouldn't go hungry. In the same way, we need a plan for interrupting our fear early. Open His Word. Phone a friend. Meet up for coffee. Don't wait until you're in fear to try and overcome fear.

Fourth, we need to reflect on God's faithfulness to us in the past.

Most of the things people worry about never happen. French philosopher Michel de Montaigne said, "My life has been full of terrible misfortunes, most of which never happened." There is now research to back this up. Researchers at Cornell University found that 85 percent of what people worry about never happens. Instead of focusing on what might be, we should turn our attention on how God has been faithful to us in the past.

My friend John has been a family friend for over 30 years. I once visited John on his farm, and he took me inside to show me his prayer journals. We sat down as he pointed out entries from 20 years ago when he specifically was praying for me. I was amazed. He also read several stories he wrote down about God's faithfulness. He said to me, "If God moves, write it down. Otherwise, you will forget, and when you need it most, it won't be there." This is great advice. In the face of fear, we need to remember the faithfulness of God.

Finally, start the day with Jesus. Meet with Jesus early in the morning and ask Him to protect you from unwanted fear. Leave no room for fear and anxiety by filling up with the goodness of God. When we go to the Lord later in the day, we usually go to Him for recovering. "Help, God!" When we seek His face in the morning, we go to Him for a fresh filling. At our church, we have encouraged people to spend the first 20 minutes of their day with Jesus.

- Read a passage of Scripture.

- Listen to a devotional podcast.

- Worship through music.

- Reflect while on a prayer walk.

BECOMING PEACEMAKERS

If you want to become a basketball player, spend time shooting hoops. If you want to become a baker, spend time baking. This is all straightforward stuff. Now apply this to peacemaking. If you want to become a peacemaker, do the things peacemakers do.

Peacemakers abide in the Lord. I love how Jesus calls Himself the vine (John 15:5). He boldly tells His disciples that they can do nothing apart from Him. This applies to us as well. When it comes to the things of God, we are helpless without Him. We are masters at building our own kingdoms; however, if we want anything to do with the Kingdom of God, we better be keen on fully surrendering to Him. If we want to carry peace into our world, we need to go to the source of peace. Through times of prayer, we will become carriers of peace.

Peacemakers learn to hear God for others. At the beginning of the COVID-19 pandemic, life was crazy. We had just decided to close the doors of the church and move to a fully online ministry. All this was uncharted territory. Many of the people in our congregation were losing their jobs and understandably frightened about their future. During this very stressful moment, my friend Thom shared a word with me that he believed God had given him for me. It was a phrase that kept coming back to him: "This is for you." I struggled to know how it applied. "What is for me?" I wondered.

Coincidentally, in my Bible reading at the time, I was in the story of Joseph. Each day I read through this story, I was more and more amazed that, even in the face of severe injustice, Joseph honored God in everything he did. I continued to reflect on Thom's word. Finally, it dawned on me. I was looking at the word completely wrong. "This is for you" was not about me. It was about Him. The Lord was asking me, like Joseph, to turn to Him and say, "This is for you."

My preaching is for you.

My parenting is for you.

My work is for you.

My worship is for you.

Everything is for you.

At the time, I was so self-focused. I was stressed with work and the demands of pastoring. But once I turned it over to Him, I experienced a great gift — His peace. A word from God brings great breakthrough.

Peacemakers step out in faith. In the story of the Good Samaritan, a man was left to die on the side of the road. Several people passed by, but the Samaritan stopped to help. When peacemakers see injustice, they don't pass by. Instead, they are generous and loving and helpful. Peacemakers don't just dream about peace or wish for peace. They make peace by standing up for others and stepping out in faith.

ONE LAST THING

Peacemakers are not always peace achievers. Even though we might do everything in our power, we may not be able to achieve peace. Peacemaking is not always easy, but it can often result in the power of God touching the earth. Do everything possible to see peace realized.

Forgive.

Love.

Serve.

But don't be discouraged if peace is still not achieved. The Apostle Paul helps us in this when he says, "If it is possible, as far as it depends on you, live at peace with everyone" (Romans 12:18).

CHAPTER EIGHT

SAY YES TO COMPASSION

"Praise be to the God and Father of our Lord Jesus Christ, the Father of compassion and the God of all comfort, who comforts us in all our troubles, so that we can comfort those in any trouble with the comfort we ourselves receive from God." **2 CORINTHIANS 1:3-4**

I've always wanted to attend one of those fancy parties where they announce you when you enter — a royal ball of sorts where a person dressed in a puffy shirt regally proclaims your presence to the gathered guests. I'm guessing this party tradition started the trend of people wanting to show up fashionably late. Everybody wants to be announced before a full house. The closest I came to an introduction like this was at my wedding, but the band director pronounced my last name wrong — so that didn't count. I wonder, if I were invited to such a party, how would I choose to be announced.

"Hear ye, Hear ye, the Rev. Dr. Brian Mowrey and his esteemed wife

Rebecca, the Duke and Duchess of New Brunswickshire."

"Introducing the honorable Mr. Brian and Rebecca Mowrey."

"Hey everyone, Brian's here with the pizza!"

I would think long and hard about how I would be announced because introductions help us know how we can relate with one another.

Moses had already been on top of the mountain with the Lord. He was given the Ten Commandments on two tablets, but Moses would shatter them on the ground — not because he was clumsy, but because he was so disappointed by what he saw when he came down the mountain. The people were worshiping a handmade idol. Out of the graciousness of God, Moses was invited back up on the mountain where God gave him a second set of tablets. Then something extraordinary happened. Much like a fancy party, God passed in front of Moses and announced Himself.

What did He say?

"Introducing, God Almighty! Creator of Heaven and earth!"

"Please welcome the all-knowing and all-powerful God!"

"Put your hands together for the Alpha and Omega, the Everlasting God!"

While any of these could be included on His resume, God passed in front of Moses and proclaimed, "The LORD, the LORD, the compassionate and gracious God" (Exodus 34:6). He could have announced Himself in an infinite number of ways, but He chose to lead with Compassion.

ANNOUNCING GOD

Who is God to you? If you were to write the story and God was entering the scene, how would you announce Him? Would you introduce Him as the God who is constantly angry? Or as the God who is keeping score?

Our view of God matters. Nobody wants to be around someone who is always in a bad mood. Keeping company with someone who is always upset and angry is no treat. Equally, we could never satisfy a God who was always keeping score. We always come up short when the goal is perfection.

But how should we view God? I would suggest that we view God the way He has chosen to announce Himself. He is the compassionate and gracious God. In 2 Corinthians 1:3, the Apostle Paul describes God as "the Father of compassion." What does it mean for God to be the Father of compassion?

I have a wonderful earthly father. One of the things that makes my dad such a good father is that he leads by example. He has shown my siblings and me what it means to love, respect others, work hard, give generously and stand for one another. God is a great father because

He leads by example. As the Father of compassion, He is always extending His grace, love and mercy to us.

THE COVERAGE OF GOD'S COMPASSION

On October 29, 2011, a nor'easter devastated New England with an unusually wet and early snowfall. The trees, still full of leaves, bowed under the weight of the massive amounts of snow. Many large trees and limbs fell to the ground, taking out power lines and cars, and severely damaging homes. We lost power at our house immediately, so I took the family to my parents' house just a few miles away. I remember driving under the canopy of cracking tree limbs above our heads praying that none would fall on our truck. We arrived safely and hunkered down for a fortnight (fancy word for two weeks). After the storm had passed and we regained power, we made our way back home and discovered a large tree had landed in our back-yard. Thankfully, it had missed the house. I pulled out my chainsaw, trimmed my beard and cleared the tree.

Several months later, we looked outside and noticed a 9-foot hole in the ground where the tree had fallen. Turns out, the tree landed directly on our septic system, cracking the tank. The first thing I thought to myself was, "Will this be covered by my insurance?" Come to find out, Becca's first thought was, "I'm so glad the kids didn't fall into the hole." Wait, that was my first thought too. But a close second was, "Will this be covered?" Unfortunately, it wasn't.

In life, we often ask, "Is it covered?" Or its close cousin, "Is it included?"

We might think this way with God as well. Can God cover my hurt, my pain, my mistakes? Does His grace cover my failure? Are there any exemptions?

We learn from 2 Corinthians 1 that God is the Father of compassion, but we also learn that He is "the God of all comfort, who comforts us in all our trouble" (2 Corinthians 1:3-4). I love that word "all." You don't have to do a long study to understand what all means. It means all. Everything is covered. No surprises. In everything, with anyone and for anything, God is our comforter. You might not think you are covered, but God is the Father of compassion and the God of all comfort.

ABOUNDING WITH COMPASSION

If your closest friends were to describe you, what would they say? Some of my friends might say that I am kind, that I am a good person or that I know my way around a chainsaw. But would they say that I abound with compassion? I'm not sure. I would like them to, because it would mean Jesus was working in and through me. Jesus has been very clear about what we are called to do. He says, "You must be compassionate, just as your Father is compassionate" (Luke 6:36 NLT). He leaves no option for us. As followers of Jesus, we must be compassionate. Thankfully, when you experience the compassion of God in your own life, you have the gift of being able to show that same kind of compassion to others. God is a great teacher. If we learn to receive His compassion, we will be filled with the ability to show that same kind of compassion to those around us.

WHAT IS COMPASSION?

Compassion is entering the suffering of others and being ready to help. In 1 John 3:18, it says, "Dear children, let's not merely say that we love each other; let us show the truth by our actions." Compassion is much more than a bleeding heart; it means actively engaging in the brokenness of our world, ready to help.

There is a great Peanuts comic strip where, in frame one, Charlie Brown and Linus notice Snoopy out in the cold shivering in his dog-house. In frame two, Charlie says to Linus, "Let's go cheer up Snoopy." In frame three, they are standing with Snoopy as they say to him, "Cheer up Snoopy." Finally, in frame four, Snoopy is still shivering outside in the cold while Charlie Brown and Linus are seen inside warming themselves by the fire.

This is not compassion.

This is simply feeling badly for someone.

Invite Snoopy in Charlie Brown!

There are many stories in Scripture that help us understand compassion. For me, two of them highlight what I call the progression of compassion. The first story is one that Jesus tells about a son who leaves his father's house and ends up losing everything. When he finally decides to return, he goes back with a well-rehearsed apology in hand. When his father sees him coming, he didn't lock the doors.

Instead, Scripture tells us, "his father **saw him** and was **filled with compassion** for him; he **ran to his son**, threw his arms around him and kissed him" (Luke 15:20).

He saw.

He felt.

He moved.

In the second story, Jesus entered a town called Nain with a great crowd following Him. While He and His disciples were walking into the city, there was a funeral procession exiting. One crowd was following the sadness of loss and death, while another crowd was following Jesus, who was bringing life wherever He went. Jesus could have let the funeral procession go by without interfering, but His heart compelled him to do something.

"When the Lord **saw her**, His **heart went out to her** and He said, 'Don't cry.' Then He **went up and touched the bier** they were carrying him on, and the bearers stood still. He said, 'Young man, I say to you, get up!' The dead man sat up and began to talk, and Jesus gave him back to his mother" (Luke 7:13-15).

He saw.

He felt.

He moved.

Jesus saw the pain and sorrow of the woman. His heart broke for her, so He moved out in compassion and did something extraordinary. This is how compassion works. To say yes to compassion means to open our eyes to the needs of others, allow ourselves to feel the pain and hurt they are experiencing, and actively move out to help.

We see.

We feel.

We move.

COMPASSION IS THE ANSWER

Every day we must ask ourselves how we are going to respond to our hurting world. How will you respond to the coworker who keeps frustrating you? How will you respond to the person who is going through tremendous loss? How will you respond to the neighbor whose loved one is struggling? How will you respond in an increasingly aggressive and divisive political world? Responding with compassion engages and activates the Kingdom of God among us.

With those who we disagree with – compassion is the answer.

With those who are hurting – compassion is the answer.

With those we don't understand – compassion is the answer.

Out of compassion, Jesus healed blind Bartimaeus. Out of compassion,

He felt great love for the rich young ruler. Out of compassion, His heart broke for the lost. And ultimately out of compassion, He went to the cross. Compassion is God's chosen way to tug on the heart strings of every believer to get them moving into the things of God.

A meteorologist depends on the readings of a barometer. He requires this instrumentation to measure atmospheric pressure to forecast the weather. Without a barometer, a meteorologist would be very limited in being able to determine what was happening in the atmosphere around him. In the same way, we rely on compassion to determine what is happening spiritually around us. Having a heart of compassion is like being able to carry around a barometer that reads the spiritual atmosphere within a situation or circumstance. Without it, we would be unable to detect how others are coping and how God is working in the unseen realm around us. But with it, we can partner with God in incredible ways.

Tom was a math teacher at a very prestigious prep school. One of his students was the governor's son, who was struggling in Tom's calculus class. Tom graciously offered to help him after school. To thank him, Tom was invited to the governor's winter ball. Donning a rented tuxedo, he pulled up to the Governor's Mansion in his Toyota Celica ready to enjoy the caviar. Just when he pulled up to the mansion, it started to pour. As he walked up to the house, the unthinkable happened. He slipped and fell into a puddle of mud. His pants and jacket were ruined, so he went back to his car in desperate search for something acceptable to wear. All he had was an old pair of jeans he wore for his side job mowing lawns. Not willing to give up on the evening, he slipped on the old jeans, tucked in his tuxedo shirt and entered the party. Like the Red Sea, the crowd parted as Tom walked in. He clearly didn't belong.

Who invited this guy?

Did he not know the dress code?

Just then the governor was coming down the stairs. He saw the disapproving looks from the people who were avoiding poor Tom. The governor immediately returned upstairs and came down a few minutes later wearing an old pair of jeans, with his tuxedo shirt tucked in. The governor went straight up to Tom, put his arm around him and spent the rest of the evening by his side. Tom became the hit of the party.

He saw.

He felt.

He moved.

GET GOING

When we say yes to compassion, the Lord empowers us. His comfort both blesses and equips us. Even when we don't feel qualified, God can use us powerfully. Usually the thing that stops me from showing compassion to others is self-doubt. I don't feel adequate. Even as a pastor, I often feel this way. What could I possibly say or do to help a person who is hurting?

I've learned that, when it comes to comforting others, usually the most difficult step is saying yes. Once we get past our own self-doubt, we can step into what God wants to do in and through us. I'm always amazed how God can use our simple yes to bring comfort and compassion to another person. Just get your feet moving, and God will show up along the way.

I remember driving over to my friend's house who had just lost his wife to a long battle with cancer. He was devastated and wanted me to come over to be with him and his two daughters. I was both honored to be asked and scared out of my mind, not knowing what I could possibly do to help. I wished I had brought something with me as a comforting gift. I looked in my truck and found one of my daughter's stuffed animals. It was a pink bunny rabbit. Even though it was a bit tattered, I dusted it off and decided to take it in for my friend's youngest daughter. I entered a home that was full of sorrow. I didn't know what to say. Eventually I turned to his little girl and said, "I brought this bunny for you. I hope you like it."

This precious girl looked up, ran over to me and wrapped her little arms around my legs. She took the bunny out of my hands and cuddled it fiercely. A week later, my friend called and thanked me for the pink bunny. He told me that every year on his daughter's birthday, his wife would buy her a pink bunny. As a family, they even called her "Bunny" as a nickname. For this little girl, when I handed her the pink bunny, she believed her mom had given her one last gift.

She knew she was going to be ok.

When we say yes to compassion, God will surprise us.

I've also learned through the years that presence is often the best thing you can offer. Too often, we think we must have all the answers. This just isn't the case. We were built for relationship and, in times of struggle, people want other people to be close. I've sat with people in the middle of the worst of tragedies and I've discovered that our presence can mean more than our words. Our presence communicates more than thousands of words ever could. The fact that you showed up will be what the person will always remember.

COMPASSION HAS A WHO

Compassion always has a "who" attached to it. When you say yes to compassion, you are saying yes to showing the love of Jesus to someone in their time of need. This leaves us with a challenge. Who is God calling you to act compassionately toward right now? Will you say yes?

I hope you get invited to one of those fancy parties where they announce your name as you enter. Remember to show up fashionably late. When they announce you, I hope they say, "Introducing [Put Your Name and Title Here (be creative)], who abounds with the compassion and comfort of Jesus."

CHAPTER NINE
SAY YES TO UNITY

"My prayer is not for them alone. I pray also for those who will believe in me through their message, that all of them may be one, Father, just as you are in me and I am in you." **JOHN 17:20-21**

Last year, my brother and I decided to spend our Saturday mornings teaching a few dozen kids how to ice skate. We had no idea that more than 200 would show up. Proud parents sent their reluctant 6-year-olds out onto the ice for their first hockey practice fully equipped with every type of padding purchasable. Most of the kids had never ice skated before. The rink was filled with screaming and crying — mostly from Craig and me.

Once on the ice, the parents had a hard time locating their child because they all looked the same suited up. Jim and Nicole had the answer. Before week two, they spray-painted a neon green dot on their daughter's helmet. Now that she was marked, they could easily locate her on the ice for those action photos they were looking for. This got me thinking. As Christians, what marks us? How should we be identified in the crowd? What is our neon green dot?

According to Jesus, it's unity in the Spirit.

If you want to know what is important to someone, listen to how he or she prays. When we pray, our hearts are revealed. If you want to know what matters most to my kids, listen to what they pray for. Quickly you will discover Pumpkin the cat's lazy eye outranks Father's Day. What we pray for is what matters most to us.

Hannah prayed for a son (1 Samuel 1).

A small congregation prayed for Peter's release (Acts 12).

Paul prayed for the churches he planted.

And Jesus prays for unity.

In John 17, Jesus prays to His Father "that they would be one, just as we are one." In case you didn't know, we are the "they" and He is the "we." Jesus' heart is that we would be one just like He and the Father are one. He prays for a divine kind of unity that allows each one of us to experience the blessed closeness shared among Father, Son and Holy Spirit. Unity matters to the Lord.

WHAT IS UNITY?

There is something unique about Christian unity. A group of people can find unity around a hobby, an entertainer or a passion for sports, like petitioning for the Whalers return to Hartford, but this is not what Jesus prayed for. The kind of unity that Jesus prayed for and ultimately was worth Him dying for is the unity found through the Holy Spirit. In his letter to the church in Ephesus, Paul writes, "Make every effort to keep the unity of the Spirit through the bond of peace" (Ephesians 4:3).

Christian unity has a source. The source is the presence of God through the gift of His Holy Spirit. Luke spoke about the early church saying, "All the believers were together and had everything in common" (Acts 2:44). He is not saying that everyone had the same haircut or rooted for the same football team. He is saying that they all shared the same Spirit and, therefore, had everything in common because Jesus was their everything. Perfect unity did not happen by replication, but by revelation. The more the Holy Spirit was revealed in and through them, the more they became united.

KEEPING IN STEP

My kids and I love going to the Labor Day Parade. They like it because of the candy that is thrown out of the fire trucks, but I like it because of the marching band. There is something about a good marching band that is so powerful and exciting.

Now to be honest, there are two different kinds of marching bands. The first is like my high school experience. No one had a complete uniform, so we had to supplement with homemade items. Our band couldn't be taken seriously when half the group was wearing white sweatpants with the school logo painted on by the ninth-grade home economics class. Although we boasted over 100 strong, only 10% knew the music. The rest of us faked it. Feels good to finally make that confession. All of us were out of step. When we rounded the corner of the street, it was like a tractor trailer careening out of control, sending every man, woman and child scrambling for safety.

The second kind of marching band is very different. When you watch the Texas Southern University Ocean of Soul Marching Band, you will notice not only do they all know the music, but they put on a halftime show that is like a flash mob on steroids. They combine intricate dance moves, acrobatics and pyrotechnics with rocking music that gets every foot stomping. It is a jaw-dropping experience for everyone in the crowd. I love this kind of marching band because, although they are all playing different instruments and different parts, when put together, the result is powerful. This is a great picture of Christian unity — all gifted in different ways, marching to the same cadence of the Spirit, powerfully revealing the love of Jesus together.

Are we marching together?

Are you in step?

For my doctoral work, the Lord led me to the topic of unity in diversity. I had no prior experience in this area. But as I stepped into this challenging work, it turned from a topic to study to what my heart now beats for. I sat with over 100 people to hear their stories and gain their wisdom on how to become a community that loves one another in the way that pleases the Lord. From this study, I discovered that the kind of unity Jesus prayed for requires us saying yes to nine commitments.

KEEP JESUS AT THE CENTER

I coach U7 girls' soccer. It's not a high paying job in case you were wondering. As a coach, I am constantly yelling out the same things every single game.

"Girls, we are going that way!"

"Girls, stop chatting!"

"Girls, spread out!"

That's about all it takes to be a U7 girls' soccer coach. Again, it doesn't pay well. Or maybe they are just getting what they paid for. It is nearly impossible to get the girls to spread out across the field. It doesn't make any sense to them. They all want to go after the ball. They would follow the ball into the town sanitation fields if that's where it rolled. They are like moths to a flame.

We should have the same tenacious pursuit. There should be nothing that keeps us from running after Jesus. His truth. His voice. His ways. His call. Unity is found when we draw our attention to Jesus and run after Him, no matter where He goes. Saying yes to unity means saying yes to radically living for Jesus.

MAKE SHARING JESUS THE MISSION

We are united to be sent out into the world. Jesus wanted the disciples to be one in their mission. Jesus prayed, "Just as you sent me into the world, I am sending them into the world" (John 17:18). When we make the mission of Jesus our mission, we step into greater unity together.

In John 17:17, Jesus prays that we would be sanctified/set apart. But for what purpose? In his commentary on the Gospel of John, theologian Edward W. Klink concludes that Jesus prayed for His disciples to be sanctified or set apart so that they would be anointed for a sacred mission: "The verb 'sanctify' (ἁγίασον) can mean 'to separate, make holy,' but in this context refers to the act of consecrating or dedicating a person for a holy task." Jesus prayed that the disciples would be set apart for a great work — that is, their "holy task" to "make disciples of all nations" (Matt. 28:19). Being set apart for this mission brought them together in unity.

My daughters end up fighting more when they have nothing to do. They are much better off when they are working on a project or playing together. I can see when tension is rising in the house among them, and I've learned to give them a task they can all work on together. Sending them out to work on a dance routine on the trampoline brings them together and relieves us of a head-to-head battle. We were created to work together and to have a shared purpose. Our mission is great — better than creating a show-stopping trampoline routine. It's to love one another and introduce people to Jesus.

ALWAYS CHOOSE LOVE

Unity happens when we commit to always love – no matter what. This can be difficult when the person hurts us or disagrees with us.

But it is the way of Jesus. And when we choose to follow the way of Jesus, we receive the blessing of Jesus. As Christ-followers, we must lead the way in love. Sadly, too many have had encounters with Christians that have led them to believe we are judgmental and unloving. Mahatma Gandhi famously said, "I like your Christ, I do not like your Christians. Your Christians are so unlike your Christ." What would it take to erase the relevance of this statement?

Generosity.

Gratitude.

Compassion.

Sacrifice.

Servant Hearts.

Humility.

Love.

I am always amazed by Jesus' love for His disciples — even when He knew they would deny Him and even worse betray Him. Just before His death, Jesus met with them in an upper room. He took a bowl and a towel and washed each of their feet. Imagine Jesus going around the circle.

Andrew.

James.

John.

Philip.

Bartholomew (Yes, he was a disciple).

Matthew.

Thomas.

Judas. No skip him!

But Jesus would not skip him. He washed Judas' feet. And I believe, if you were in that circle, He would have washed your feet too. Why? Because He loves you. In our sin and in our failure, He would have washed our feet. This is the commitment we are to make as well — to always choose love. Saying yes to unity means saying yes to a new standard of love.

HONOR ONE ANOTHER

Part of my research for my doctoral work was listening to people's stories. I was so amazed by their willingness to let me into their lives and share their greatest moments of joy as well as their deepest hurts. The Lord brought a great revelation to me through this process.

I learned that honor brings healing.

When a person is honored for who they are in the Lord, hurts move from open wounds to scars. There is power in honoring a person. It means so much when a person recognizes our worth and speaks it over us. Think of those times in your life when someone else acknowledged your unique purpose in this world and honored you for it. When we honor others, it is like depositing gold into their spiritual account. It encourages them and gives them confidence in who they are in the Lord. In the same way, we can honor a person's position and potential. We can encourage people for who they are, and what they are accomplishing. But also, and maybe more importantly, we can honor them by helping them achieve their potential.

Jennifer told me that for 20 years she felt like she never belonged. She was one of the only black students in a mainly white school. Her family was different from all her friends. They ate different things and talked about different topics. They faced different challenges. Many of her classmates made fun of her for no reason besides the color of her skin. Always the outsider, Jennifer lost confidence in herself.

Now in her forties, Jennifer is a strong confident woman who runs a large organization. I asked her if she remembered when and how she gained her confidence back. She told me it happened her senior year of college. A fellow student named Megan, who she didn't know very well, came up to her and shared a powerful word of encouragement. Jennifer loved helping the students with disabilities. She would always help her friends in wheelchairs with their food trays through the cafeteria, and when she walked through the halls, she was usually helping someone with their backpack. When Jennifer was honored in this way, she told me it changed her life forever. She now leads an organization that provides care for people with disabilities. She couldn't be happier because she is living a life of purpose. She attributes that breakthrough because of one girl's choice to honor her. Megan noticed Jennifer's compassion for the students with disabilities and encouraged her by saying, "God has given you a special love for our friends with disabilities. I think He is going to use you to bless them and care for them and make sure they know they are loved."

This word of honoring changed Jennifer's life. Through Megan, God had pointed out Jennifer's purpose. She now is the president of a large organization that meets the needs of those with disabilities. And Jennifer could not be happier. Everything changed through a moment of honoring.

Honor brings healing. If we want to be united, we must learn how to honor one another.

FORGIVE ONE ANOTHER

Read Chapter 6 again! Just kidding. I often say at a wedding ceremony that the greatest way to love your spouse is by loving Jesus first. The reason is because, when you love Jesus first, you will learn firsthand the importance of forgiveness. And forgiveness will be necessary in any marriage and relationship. We are going to hurt one another. Plan on it. Offenses will happen. But how we respond is our choice. If we want to be united, we need to commit to forgive one another.

Are you withholding forgiveness? Jesus' heart for us is to be one. It's time to forgive. It's time to let go of the offense and allow God to begin to restore you.

FEAST ON THE WORD OF GOD

I recently learned that what you eat matters. I was living my life eating whatever I wanted, and it showed! Maybe not as much on the outside, but my insides were aching. Damage was being done. If we want to be united, we must be conscious of what we are feeding ourselves. A steady diet of social media, gossip magazines, alarmist news and office grumbling will not lead us to love one another – at least it doesn't for me. These distractions are not going to foster the kind of unity that Jesus prayed for.

The Word of God is what brings us life. If we want to desire unity more naturally, we must feast on the Word of God. The Word of God aligns our hearts to His and inspires us to live like Jesus.

NEVER REACH EMPTY

Some people love to run their gas gauge as low as it will go. It thrills them to see the needle on the other side of "E." You know who you are. When it comes to the things of the Lord, this habit does not work in our favor. If we want to be united, we need to be filled.

The Spirit of Christ Jesus unites us. If we are empty, we have no real chance for the kind of unity Jesus prays for. To be united means making a commitment to being filled each day by the power of the

Holy Spirit. I would encourage you to ask the Lord to fill you each morning. First thing.

CHOOSE TO WALK TOGETHER

All of us have a friend who takes some effort. Maybe I'm that friend. But when we choose to love and walk with them, it is a blessing. Unity is chosen. It takes us deliberately and intentionally working to walk together. It won't always be easy, but it brings great glory to the Lord. And more often than not, when you choose to show someone love, you end up loving them.

Unity happens when we decide to live life together. Sit with people and listen to their stories. Share meals and grow in fellowship with each other. Be intentional about befriending all kinds of people. Commit to being the body of Christ together. Learn about each other and fight for one another. Commit to learning about another person's world view. Do your best to experience what it is like to walk in their shoes. Throw out assumption and begin to build relationships that will honor the Lord's heart for unity in diversity.

PRAY FIRST

We can react or we can respond. It's better to be a responder. Reactors speak out, act out and move out without thinking. This usually ends with the need for an apology. If we want to be people who carry peace and cultivate unity, we need to pray first. Instead of reacting, we need to respond after seeking wisdom from the Lord. We have the greatest counselor of all time. Shouldn't we consult Him?

Jesus Himself would go off on His own to pray. We too must pray first. Be equipped and empowered through prayer for every moment you enter. When we are prayed up, we have a great chance to grow in unity together, even in the hard stuff.

It's time to march together — not like my high school band, but instead like the Texas Southern University Ocean of Soul Marching Band. Let's honor one another for the parts we each play. Let's love one another with the love of Jesus. And let's walk in step with the Spirt together for God's glory.

CHAPTER TEN

SAY YES TO GRATITUDE

"Give thanks in all circumstances; for this is God's will for you in Christ Jesus." **1 THESSALONIANS 5:18**

This might be hard for you to believe, but I can't bench press 300 pounds. Even more shocking is that I can't bench press 500 pounds. If I were to try and lift 300 pounds, the weight would fall on my neck and crush me. I would be desperate for someone to come and rescue me. If I were to try and lift 500 pounds, the weight would do the same thing — fall on my neck and crush me. I would be in the same position as I was with the 300 pounds and desperate for someone to come and help me. Now, let's say that in both situations someone came to my rescue and lifted the bar off my neck. Would I be more thankful to the person who lifted the 300 pounds or the 500 pounds?

Jesus asked the same question of a man named Simon (Luke 7:36-50). The story was a bit different, but the question was the same. Jesus told Simon a story about two people who were in debt. One was in debt 50 coins and the other was in debt 500 coins. Jesus makes it clear to Simon that neither could pay off the debt. They are both in the same position, unable to pay off the money lender. The good news is that the money lender decides to free them both of their debt. Then Jesus asks, "Who would love the money lender more?" Simon believed the one who had been forgiven more would love more. Jesus then responds in an interesting way. He says, "You have judged correctly." The problem was that Jesus wasn't asking Simon to be the judge. Instead, He was hoping Simon would put himself in the shoes of the indebted and take on a posture of gratitude.

Let's go back to my weightlifting. Would I be more thankful to the person who lifted the 300 pounds or the 500 pounds? The amount of weight doesn't matter. I'm in the same perilous predicament regardless. The degree of my gratitude would not be measured by the amount of the weight but by the mere gift of the rescue.

Imagine laying on the weight bench caught under the load of the bar. There is no chance of lifting the weight on your own power. Your windpipe is collapsing as you gasp for air. Your eyes are frantically looking for someone to rescue you. Now imagine seeing someone through blurred vision approaching you. The weight is lifted and air returns to your lungs.

How would you respond?

There was another person in attendance when Jesus was with Simon. We don't know her name, but she sat at Jesus' feet weeping and washing His feet. She was a known sinner in the community. How she made her way this close to Jesus we don't know. She had clearly been transformed by Jesus. Maybe she had heard Him talk about the forgiveness of sins. Maybe she had responded to the call to follow Him. Either way, she was worshiping Jesus because she had been deeply affected by Him.

I wonder, was she 50 coins in debt or 500?

I'm sure Simon thought she was at least 500 coins in debt. He could have easily judged her situation correctly. But that doesn't matter. What really matters is that she had been forgiven a debt she couldn't pay, and now she was responding to the amazing grace of Jesus in her life. Her heart overflowed with thanks. This is the good news of the Gospel. All of us have been forgiven a great debt. It doesn't matter the amount. None of us could pay it off. But we have been forgiven anyway. Out of the grace of God and through the death and resurrection of Jesus, our debt has been paid. The crushing weight of our sin has been lifted. The real question becomes, "How will we respond?"

Hannah prayed for a child and when the Lord blessed her with a son, she returned to the Lord and gave thanks (1 Samuel 2). When Jesus healed 10 lepers, only one returned to thank Him (Luke 17:11-19). He praised the Lord in a loud voice and Jesus commended him for his faith. Will you be that one? Will you respond with gratitude?

THE IMPORTANCE OF SAYING YES TO GRATITUDE

Health Benefits

In the Harvard Health Publishing article, "Giving thanks can make you happier," the author strongly attributes thanksgiving as a major contributor to a person's happiness and well-being, saying, "In positive psychology research, gratitude is strongly and consistently associated with greater happiness. Gratitude helps people feel more positive emotions, relish good experiences, improve their health, deal with adversity, and build strong relationships." Based on the research of Dr. Robert A. Emmons of the University of California, and Dr. Michael E. McCullough of the University of Miami, their studies have found that gratitude leads to lower risk of falling into despair, greater happiness, increased sense of fulfillment, positive relationships and better sleep. But wait, there's more. According to a study in the Journal of Theoretical Social Psychology, feeling grateful toward your partner and vice versa can improve numerous aspects of your relationship, including feelings of connectedness and overall satisfaction as a couple. And there are hundreds of studies just like these.

A Right State of Mind

What we focus on grows. When we fixate on rejection, failure becomes our identity. When we're centered on the hurt, we can miss the healing. When we are blinded by the problem, we will never see the solution. But if you focus on the things of the Lord, it will lead you to joy and hope. Thankfulness begins with the choice to focus on the right things. The Apostle Paul encourages us in this way, "Finally, brothers and sisters, whatever is true, whatever is noble, whatever is right, whatever is pure, whatever is lovely, whatever is admirable — if anything is excellent or praiseworthy — think about such things" (Philippians 4:8). Paul knew that, when we think on these things, we will be led to gratitude.

Sadly, when we are not thanking, we are usually complaining. And we are good at complaining. For many, it's a core competency. This is exactly where the evil one wants us — grumbling, griping and totally distracted from our real mission of building the Kingdom of God. When we are complaining, we are self-focused and not Kingdom-focused. Complaining is a trap. This is why giving thanks is a powerful weapon in spiritual warfare. It gives us the right attitude. The right focus. The right state of mind.

Act of Worship

We should give thanks because it's an act of worship. Only one of the 10 lepers, after noticing that he was healed, came back to Jesus saying, "Praise God!" This one man fell at Jesus' feet thanking Him for what He had done. Jesus asked him, "Didn't I heal 10 men? Where are the other nine? Has no one returned to give glory to God except this one?" Only one of the men completed the story by praising God through thanks. And notice the result of this one man's gratitude — it brought glory to God. His thanks became an offering of worship to the Lord.

You can hear the disappointment in Jesus' voice after seeing that only one returned. I can imagine Jesus thinking, "I've done this great thing for them, and they have so quickly forgotten me. They received what they wanted, so now they no longer have a need for me." I'm sure God's heart has broken many times over my lack of returning to give thanks. Thanksgiving is the necessary response to who God is to us, what He has done for us, and what he continues to do through us each day. When we return to Jesus and thank Him for His goodness to us, we worship Him. We bring Him glory! Let us not forget to return.

Becca and I try hard to teach our kids to be grateful. Surprisingly, this feature does not come built in. We are continually reminding them to give thanks. There was one season where we were laying this lesson on thick. Finally, we saw some breakthrough. We took the girls out for dinner and Bria, who was 6 at the time, came to us and said, "Papa and Mama, thank you for dinner. I know it cost you like sixty-five hundred-thousand dollars." This warmed my heart, despite my concern for Bria's math skills. Her gratitude blessed me. This is what happens when we turn to the Lord and thank Him. It is worship. It warms His heart. Have you remembered to turn back to Jesus and give Him thanks? It's not too late.

Becoming Thankful

I often pray this prayer over a couple at their wedding, "God we ask that today would mark the day that John and Judy love each other the least." My hope is that as time passes their love will grow. I would pray this prayer for your relationship with Jesus as well — that you would grow in your love of Jesus as you get to know Him more and more. Thankfulness arises from knowing — not just learning. You can learn all about the Lord and still not know Him. Learning should always be done for the purpose of knowing. When we grow in know-ing Jesus, the natural result will be to thank and praise Him. If you want to become more thankful, then pursue knowing Jesus.

Another way to grow a heart of gratitude is through practice. Giving thanks spurs on a heart of thanksgiving. I remember when R.T. Kendall spoke at our church on giving thanks. He challenged our church to give thanks for five things every night before bed. As I drove him to the airport, he said, "Brian, if your congregation takes this seriously, they will start by thanking God for five things. Then it will quickly become 10. And before you know it, they will fall asleep thanking the Lord for the countless ways He has blessed them." If you want to be thankful, then start by giving thanks.

We can also grow our hearts of gratitude by saying, "Thank you." The call is to give thanks, not just feel thankful. I love in Scripture when Mary the mother of Jesus thanks the Lord. She sings. I love how Hannah thanks the Lord. She bursts into song. One way to grow our thankfulness is by saying something – or singing something – or writing something. Don't hold your gratitude in. Be thankful and say so. When you write that letter or give that word of encouragement to a friend, it will fan the flame of gratitude within you.

In his book, "The Mayo Clinic Guide to Stress Free Living," Dr. Amit Sood emphasizes the importance of practicing thankfulness. He concluded that, if we start our day with thankfulness and learn to be thankful for the little things, we will become more grateful people. Seeing the goodness of God in the little things will help us develop a lifestyle of thanksgiving. It's even good to thank God for the not so fun parts of life.

"Let's Be Thankful"

For the alarm that goes off in the early morning,
because it means that I am alive.

For the taxes that I pay,
because it means that I am employed.

For all the complaining I hear about the government,
because it means that we have freedom of speech.

For the lawn that needs mowing, windows that need cleaning,
gutters that need fixing, because it means I have a home.

For the clothes that fit a little too snug,
because it means I have more than enough to eat.

For my heating bills, because it means I am warm.

For weariness and aching muscles at the end of the day,
because it means that I have been capable of hard work.

And even for the mess to clean after a party
because it means that I have been surrounded by friends!

The Good News Paper, May 2005

It would be easy to pass by the little blessings in life. If we want to become more thankful, we need to have our eyes open to the goodness of God in our step-by-step walk with Him.

Another way we can grow in gratitude is by thanking God even when things aren't finished. When you think of the creation story, God paused several times, looked at what He created and saw that it was good. Think about it. The first day He created light. He stepped back and saw that it was good. There was no vegetation yet, no animals, no water – His creation was very much in process. But God saw the goodness in the light. We too need to be able to see things as good – even when they are not fully finished. We need to remember to pause along the road of life and say thanks to the Lord. What in your life is still in process? Will you thank the Lord for how He is moving, even though He hasn't brought it to completion yet?

REASONS TO BE THANKFUL

Julie had Lou Gehrig's disease. Toward the end of her life, she lost the ability to speak, so she used a computer to communicate. When I visited Julie, she would always share the reasons she was thankful. She was thankful for her computer, which allowed her to connect with others. She was thankful for the bed we brought her that lifted her up so she could see the TV. She was thankful for the visitors she had. She was thankful for the meals that were prepared for her. She was thankful for the staff who looked after her. For a woman who appeared to have nothing to be thankful for, she brought us through a master class on gratitude. She always had something to be thankful for. Even until her last breath – she was thankful she was going to see Jesus.

Compared to Julie, we are all far behind. We have some catching up to do. Let's become more thankful by being more thankful.

Will you say yes?

CHAPTER ELEVEN

SAY YES TO GENEROSITY

"Each of you should give what you have decided in your heart to give, not reluctantly or under compulsion, for God loves a cheerful giver." **2 CORINTHIANS 9:7**

We had a long weekend off from school during my university's fall break, so a few of my buddies and I traveled north to Duluth, Minnesota, where my friend John lived. The drive up I-35 took us three hours, or at least that's what we told his parents. I can't remember. What I do remember was the briefing John gave us before entering his house. He turned off the car, locked the doors and adjusted the rearview mirror like a middle school bus driver reprimanding the delinquents misbehaving in the back seats. With our seat belts securely fastened, John gravely listed off the banned topics of conversation.

His brother's new tattoo.

His uncle's off-color jokes.

His sister's boyfriend.

And the granddaddy of them all — the Dallas North Stars.

All were taboo.

Once in the house, all I wanted to talk about was his brother's new face tattoo. Every family has these lists of topics that are off-limits. This chapter is going to enter the no-fly zone. Sit down and fasten your seat belt.

How are you investing your time? How are you spending your money? Wait. Don't skip to the next chapter. It's time to talk about saying yes to generosity.

MY GIVING STORY

I grew up in a family that was always very generous. My parents were generous to us, to their church and with their friends. They modeled well what it looks like to give of their time and resources to things that really matter. As I entered my young adult years, I learned that it was one thing to watch someone be generous and an entirely different thing to be generous yourself.

Shortly after our wedding, Becca and I sat down and made a plan for giving generously as a couple. Both of our families had modeled this well for us, and we saw how God had done great things through their generosity, so we wanted to do the same. We decided to give 10 percent of our income. It was the first check that came out of our account each pay period. At first, it was painful to watch the dollars go out of my account. Paying the mortgage would have been easier, and our dates could have been fancier. There were so many things I could do with that money. I would look for reasons to keep those dollar bills.

A little boy was given two dollars. His father told him, "You can do anything you want with the one dollar, but the other one belongs to the Lord." The little boy, full of excitement, ran to the toy store holding both dollars in his hand. On the way, he tripped, and one of the dollars slipped from his hand. It flew high into the sky and then floated down directly over a storm drain. The boy couldn't get up fast enough to catch George Washington before he slipped through the grate and disappeared. He pulled himself off the ground, looked up to the sky and said, "Well Lord, there goes your dollar." You can always find a reason why the one dollar left in your hand is yours, and the one you thought you had was His.

Over the years, the Lord has grown my heart for giving. Change began when we said yes. I stopped giving out of obligation and started giving out of worship, and God has forever transformed me.

THE PRINCIPLES OF GENEROSITY

I did a study on some of the most used words in the Bible. I discovered that the word "believe" is used 289 times throughout Scripture. You can find the word "pray" 367 times and the word "love" 686 times. You would think these are the most popular words in the Bible. But there is one that beats them all. The word "give" appears 1,433 times. But why?

First, we find the word give so often because our God is a giver. We serve a generous God and Scripture talks about Him in this way. Second, give shows up so frequently because we are called to be generous people, and the generous life is the greatest life.

For generosity to become a part of the fabric of who we are, there must be reasons for generous living beyond, "Because the Bible says so." Acting in obedience to what the Bible says will guide you in the right direction, but it is helpful to know the principles behind the command. The Apostle Paul outlines the principles of giving in 2 Corinthians 9:6-15. He writes this letter to strengthen the newly established church in Corinth by sowing important lessons into their lives.

You Reap What You Sow

Paul uses the culturally familiar analogy of farming by calling attention to a basic agricultural truth. A farmer who sows seed sparingly will reap a small harvest, but a farmer who sows generously will reap a large one. This principle applies to our spiritual life as well. If we want to experience spiritual growth, we must invest in the things of God. Nothing happens until you plant the seed. If you want to become healthier, you must invest in working out and learning how to eat well. If you don't invest, the pants still won't fit. In the same way, if you want to see change in your spiritual life, you need to invest in godly things. Look back at the previous chapters. Each of these are areas that you can choose to plant seeds and see godly fruit. Spend time in prayer and fasting. Desire and work toward unity. Meet the needs of the most vulnerable. When these seeds are planted, they reap a great harvest for the Lord.

From this principle, we also learn that what you plant you will harvest. If you plant grass seed, you will reap grass — most of the time. If you plant tomato seeds, you will harvest tomatoes. Galatians 6:7 says, "You will reap exactly what you plant." If you sow seeds of hatred and revenge, expect to reap the same in return. But if you invest in the things of God, you can expect to reap the fruit that only God can produce.

A Matter of the Heart

The Apostle Paul has much to say about the way we are to give. We are not to give sparingly, reluctantly or in response to pressure. Instead, we are to give generously and deliberately. He calls us to "give what you have decided in your heart to give" (2 Corinthians 9:7). The call is to consult our heart – that is, to go before the Lord and allow Him to speak to us about our giving. Paul is calling us to give from the heart as an outpouring of inward transformation and joy in the Lord. Generosity, no matter the genre or mode, is the physical outworking of an inner reality. When we are generous, it is a demonstration of a deep understanding of what we have already received in the Lord. If you want to know where your heart is, take inventory of your generosity.

Give Cheerfully

Giving our time or resources is not done out of obligation or pressure but is done cheerfully. I once went to a fancy restaurant and was surprised to find that, when I went into the bathroom, there was a guy sitting on a folding chair in a tuxedo waiting for me. When I went to wash my hands, he offered me a towel. I thanked him and then realized I was supposed to leave a tip. So I did. I've washed my own hands plenty of times without the assistance of anyone else. And I don't say that to brag. I tipped him only because it was the thing to do. Is this why we give to the Lord? Because it's the thing to do. If you don't give something, you might be considered stingy or even worse, ungodly. So, you give a little something to clear your conscience and prove your commitment to the strangers in your pew. Generosity might start as obligation, but this is not where the Lord wants us to stay. Giving is done best cheerfully. Right at the center of Paul's teaching, he says, "God loves a cheerful giver" (2 Corinthians 9:7). When we give out of a heart of thanksgiving and with a desire to be involved in the things of God, we can easily give with a cheerful heart because we get to bring a gift to the Lord!

God Is Trustworthy

Generosity requires trusting in the Lord. One of the reasons God commands us to give is so that we can learn about Him. Through the tangible act of giving to the Lord, we are saying, "Lord I trust you." And this opens the door for God to prove His faithfulness to us. When we place our trust in Him, His faithfulness is revealed in return.

As we were pushing our first daughter in her stroller, Becca and I were on a walk together, and we began wondering if it was time for me to go to seminary. We were overwhelmed by the thought because of the cost both in time and money. Yet, we felt strongly that God was calling us to this next step. Without knowing how we would pay for it, I applied and was accepted. Just before we had to make the first payment, Becca was asked by some of our close friends to represent them as their realtor. This was a side gig for Becca. She found them a home and her commission check covered the first year of seminary, including books.

God Is the Source

It's very important to humbly acknowledge where everything comes from. My kids often mistakenly believe that they have their own room. I quickly remind them it is their Mom and Dad's room and they get to use it. God is the giver and keeper of time. God is the one who gives us everything we have — so I guess my girls' rooms are actually His. The Apostle Paul reminds us that the seed in the farmer's hand comes from God. The farmer would have nothing to sow if God had not provided the seeds to plant. And without the seed, there is no harvest. This is true for us as well. He gave us our abilities, strengths and opportunities. He sustains us with air to breathe and food to eat. When we give back to the Lord, we are acknowledging Him as the source of all things.

Giving Means Partnership

When we choose to be generous with what we have, we enter into a partnership with the Lord. I love when God asks Moses what is in his hand. All Moses had was a staff; however, once given to the Lord, it became a mighty instrument for His Kingdom.

After listening to the story of a missionary, my father-in-law, Ken, was so moved that he gave a donation. The missionary had a vision to start a school that would train and equip people to share the Gospel message. This was a dangerous task because Christians were being persecuted in his country. Ken was amazed by this man's boldness and chose to invest in this vision.

Seventeen years had passed, and Ken was now on an unrelated missions' trip. One afternoon, his group stopped for a meal in an off the beaten path town. While they were waiting for the food, Ken overheard two men talking. His attention was drawn to their accents because they sounded like they were from Newcastle, Pennsylvania, where he had spent several years growing up. Ken decided to approach the men to find out more about them.

"You sound like you are from Western Pennsylvania. Have you ever been to Newcastle?" he asked.

"Can I ask who you are?" one of the men responded.

"I'm Ken Owen."

Upon hearing this, the man began to smile and asked him about his three brothers and father, all of whom he named. Ken was amazed that, in such a remote place, he bumped into a man who knew his family.

The man talked fondly of living in Newcastle and remembered playing golf with Ken's dad but had moved over 20 years ago to serve the Lord in this town.

"Have you ever been involved in helping this country before?" he asked Ken.

Ken was reminded of the gift he had given nearly 17 years earlier and said, "Yes, a while back I helped a missionary start a school, but I'm not sure what happened."

The man looked Ken dead in the eyes and told him the exact amount he had given 17 years earlier.

"How did you know that?" Ken asked.

"Because I'm the person who built the school. It's in this town. Do you want to go and see it?"

Generosity builds schools.

Houses the homeless.

Feeds the hungry.

Heals the sick.

Rescues the most vulnerable.

And impacts the Kingdom of God.

What is in your hand? What has God entrusted you with? When we turn these things over to the Lord, they can be used powerfully for the Kingdom of God.

THE BARRIERS TO GENEROSITY

In Mark 10:17-22, we read of a man who came up to Jesus, knelt in front of Him and asked, "Good teacher, what must I do to inherit eternal life?" Jesus responded by listing off six of the 10 commandments:

- You must not murder.

- You must not commit adultery.

- You must not steal.

- You must not testify falsely.

- You must not cheat anyone.

- You must honor your mother and father.

The young man became ecstatic because he had done all these things. Then Jesus looked at him with love in His heart and told the young man there was still one more thing he had to do. He had to sell all his possessions, give the money to the poor and follow Jesus.

He walked away sad.

The barriers that kept this young man from following Jesus are the same barriers that keep us from living wholeheartedly for Jesus.

BARRIER NO. 1: HE ALREADY HAD A KING.

The young man believed there was something more valuable than

Jesus. He walked away from Jesus because he already had a king, and he wasn't willing to dethrone his possessions in order to follow Jesus. If we are not living for Jesus, we are living for something else. Every person on the planet is ruled by something.

A relationship.

A hobby.

A dream.

The question becomes, "What or who will be king of your life?"

BARRIER NO. 2: HE COULDN'T RELEASE CONTROL.

The young man's possessions possessed him. They had complete control over him, and he couldn't release them to follow Jesus. Often, the thing that keeps us from following Jesus completely is our unwillingness to release control. To live generously, we must trust the Lord with everything. This is a life of complete freedom, but it only comes once we decide to lay down our need to control everything we have and want. This is why we give. We are making a statement to the Lord. We are telling Him that we have put Him in charge of our lives.

BARRIER NO 3: HE COULDN'T SEE PAST THE SACRIFICE.

I'm pretty sure that, if my wife couldn't see past the pain of child-birth, our family would be much smaller. But once she was able to hold the treasure that laid beyond the suffering, she was able to fully understand how the joy outweighed the sacrifice. We often don't give because we can't see past what we are giving up. Jesus went to the cross knowing there was great victory beyond the grave. This is true in our giving as well. In our surrender to the Lord, we need to be able to look beyond the cost to see the blessing of generosity. Saying yes to generosity leads to spiritual growth and the blessing of advancing the Kingdom of God.

THE PATHWAY TO GENEROSITY

There is a pathway to a more generous life. These are things we can all do to refine and grow in generosity.

- **Resist comparing yourself with others:** When we begin comparing what we have with what others have, it always leads to greed and discontentment.

- **Rejoice in what you do have:** Give thanks to the Lord for how He has blessed you. All of us have things we can be thankful for.

- **Return an offering to the Lord:** Make generosity a habit by returning to the Lord a portion of what He has given you. Start with something consistently.

- **Respond to the needs of others:** Regularly ask God to reveal the needs of those around you, and be prepared to respond.

- **Restore margin in your life:** Create margin in your life so that you can spontaneously act generously.

A NEW PERSPECTIVE ON GENEROSITY

One Saturday, while visiting relatives in Minnesota, my family attended our niece's seventh birthday party. We found her the perfect board game that would be fun for us all to play. With this gift, I knew I would be up for uncle of the year. It was a huge success. She gave out big hugs all around. Three days later, we attended my nephew's party with the same people in attendance. When it was time to open presents, my niece handed him a gift. She had clearly wrapped it herself in some old newspaper found around the house — how cute. When did she find the time? As the wrapping came off, so did my smile. Without guilt or shame, she had regifted the present we gave her just three days earlier.

I was upset.

How could she do this?

Did she not know we would be here?

Did she not care about my feelings?

I felt betrayed.

God is never hurt when we regift something He has given us. In fact, He gave it to you to give away. Too often, we look at generosity as giving something up that we have earned.

Our money.

Our gifts.

Our time.

This just isn't the case. Generosity is more like regifting something you have been given.

His money.

His gifts.

His time.

Our role is to look for opportunities to regift things. Has the Lord gifted you with a full bank account? Terrific! What a wonderful privilege it will be for you to steward that money for the Kingdom of God. Has the Lord blessed you with a great ability to play music? Great! What a joy it will be to use that to bless the Lord. Has He given you special abilities to coordinate, host, manage, lead, inspire, build or help? Fantastic! Regift it!

Acts Chapter 2 tells the story of the early church. This was a community that was so generous there were no needs among them. Imagine that. They were extremely generous. Radically generous. I love what this led to for their community. Scripture tells us that they were glad and filled with joy. This extreme generosity led to happiness.

Be Generous. Be joyful.

CHAPTER TWELVE
SAY YES TO BEING SENT

"As you go, proclaim this message: 'The Kingdom of Heaven has come near.' Heal the sick, raise the dead, cleanse those who have leprosy, drive out demons. Freely you have received; freely give." **MATTHEW 10:7-8**

Attending an NFL football game is much different from watching it in your living room. At home you usually don't have to wait 20 minutes to go to the bathroom and you save 50 bucks on the nachos. But from inside the stadium, you're able to watch the coaches quickly substitute players seamlessly. Every player knows their exact role, and when their number is called, they are ready. You never see a kicker on the field yelling to the sideline, "Why am I out here? What do you want me to do?" It just doesn't happen. When the kicker is sent, he knows exactly why he is on the field. He was sent to kick the football.

The coach has called your number.

As Christians, we are being sent by Jesus to continue His work on earth. This is a high calling, but we can be assured that God will always be with us as we serve Him. God is unfailingly and unconditionally committed to us, and we are to be unwaveringly committed to His call on our lives to bring light into a dark world.

Our church hosts a Family Festival in October each year. The idea is to design a safe place for families to dress up and have fun, and for the church to open its doors to the community. There are prizes, games, bounce houses and face painting. One year, they held a competition for the best group costume. My four daughters decided to dress up as minions, the little yellow guys from the movie "Despicable Me." To create a more authentic portrayal of the characters, they asked me to dress up as Gru, the minion's leader. One of Gru's most prominent features is his giant bald head. Hoping to win the group prize, my girls asked — nay demanded — that I shave my head. I said no. One of my daughters said, "I mean come on Papa, how committed are you to this?"

The answer of course was, "Not very."

This is the question on the table right now. How committed are you to following Jesus? He's asking you to surrender your whole life, not just your hair. This call includes devoting our lives to leading others into deeper relationship with the Lord. It's the greatest mission. It's not the easiest, but it is certainly the most fulfilling. Jesus Himself knows what it is like to be sent. He modeled perfectly what it looks like to be sent on God's mission for the world. And now He is calling us to "Go and make disciples of all nations" (Matthew 28:19).

Will you say yes to being sent?

THE TIME IS NOW

Three men were told by Jesus to follow Him (Luke 9:57-62). The first man told Jesus, "I will follow you wherever you go." The second man said, "Lord, first let me go and bury my father." Seems like a reasonable thing to do. And the third man said, "I will follow you, Lord, but first let me go back and say goodbye to my family." Again, a reasonable request.

Jesus' response is startling. He says, "No one who puts a hand to the plow and looks back is fit for service in the Kingdom of God." I wonder how many times the disciples scratched their heads after Jesus spoke. What was Jesus' point? I thought we were talking about following Him. Did he just change the subject from ministry to agriculture? These seem like harsh words from Jesus, but He is making an important statement about commitment.

Looking back leads to returning back.

Jesus knew if they looked back, they would not move forward with Him. He wanted them to be all in. This is the call on our lives as well. Yet, we often become "but first" people in our walk with Jesus. I'll follow you Lord, but first ...

But first let me graduate.

But first let me receive the promotion.

But first let me see where this relationship goes.

But first let me do things my way.

But first let me get everything in order.

But first let me grow a bit older.

But first let me...

And Jesus' response is ... no. The time is now. Just before Jesus sends out the 72 disciples, He tells them, "The harvest is plentiful, but the workers are few" (Luke 10:2). It's time to get going. A great harvest is waiting to be gathered. The Lord has much to do in and through us. It's time to drop the "but first" attitude with a "Him first" faith.

I love the story of Ruth. After a series of major losses, Ruth decides to remain committed to her mother-in-law, even though it would mean turning from her hometown and stepping into a new life. Her commitment to Naomi determined her direction. She could have easily turned back to her hometown, Moab, but she had a new commitment that guided her life.

Each of us also has the choice to turn back to the safety and familiarity of Moab.

Back to old friendships.

Back to old addictions.

Back to old patterns of life.

Back to old fears.

Will we return to Moab? Will we look back from the plow? Or, like Ruth, will we turn to Jesus and say, "Where you go, I will go" (Ruth 1:16). Like Isaiah, will we say, "Here am I. Send me" (Isaiah 6:8).

WE ARE BEING SENT.

Like the 72 disciples, we too are being sent by Jesus, and we have a great mission. We are being sent to share the Good News of Jesus with all people. Our mission is to introduce people to the Jesus who has changed our lives. It's to show the love and compassion of Jesus and to walk with people in their faith journey.

We step into this call because we are compelled by His love to be a part of helping others step into a relationship with Him. When you know the love of Jesus, you want others to experience His love as well. You might be scared or nervous to share your faith — that is natural. But it would be unnatural to know the love of God and not want others to experience it for themselves. His love is just too good to keep to ourselves.

Dave Ayres worked as a building operator at Coca-Cola Coliseum in Toronto, which is the home arena for the Toronto Marlies, an American Hockey League team. He was also the emergency backup goalie to the backup goalie for NHL games played at the Toronto Maple Leafs' stadium. Usually he was on the ice as the Zamboni driver, not a player. However, on February 22, 2020, the goalie and the backup goalie for the Carolina Hurricanes were injured, leaving only one option – the 42-year-old Zamboni driver. Dave was nervous but he was ready. He signed a one-day contract with the Hurricanes in the locker room, put on his pads and entered the game. Before he could blink, two pucks slipped past him into the goal. Things were not looking good, but one of the pros encouraged him to just have fun. From that moment, he stopped every shot and led the team to victory. His goalie stick is now in the Hockey Hall of Fame.

Are you ready to be sent in? Maybe you feel like you have been on the sidelines for years. Maybe you are uneasy because you feel ill-equipped and unqualified, just like the Zamboni driver. God is calling you in to be the light of the world — not by your effort and might, but through the power of His Spirit.

THE MISSION IS NOT EASY.

In Luke 10:3, Jesus says, "Go, I am sending you out like lambs among wolves." I'm not trying to scare you, but it is important to understand the mission is not always easy. We need to be aware that, as we go out and share the Good News of Jesus, our enemy takes notice. Our enemy is not social media, the friend who gets under our skin or the boss's kid who got the promotion over us. Our enemy is the evil one. Our battle is not against flesh and blood but against the spiritual forces of evil in this world.

It's important that, as we are sent out, we go with the proper armor on. It would be good to familiarize yourself with Ephesians Chapter 6. We praise God that we are on the winning side, but we must expect to take some punches along the way.

Jeff was my roommate in college. He was a big guy who played on the football team. I remember him coming back from an away game one night. He had a huge cut on his forehead, and his face was all beat up. I asked him sarcastically, "How did the game go?" It looked like we had lost badly. With a smile on his face, he looked back at me and said, "We won!" We are on the winning side, but this does not mean we won't get bruised along the way.

JESUS WILL FULFILL HIS END OF THE DEAL.

The year was 1932 and the New York Yankees were playing against the Chicago Cubs in the World Series. It was game three and the score was tied four to four in the ninth inning when the Yankees greatest slugger came to the plate – Babe Ruth. The Great Bambino, the Sultan of Swat, the Caliph of Clout watched strike one pass by without swinging the bat. Just before the second pitch, he would do something no one had ever done before and no one has done since. He picked up his bat and pointed to the center field fence. Call it prophetic, call it arrogant, he was calling his shot. In Babe Ruth fashion, he was confidently predicting a home run to center field. The second pitch was delivered. Strike two. He raised his bat and pointed over the center field fence for a second time. The third pitch was delivered. Crack! Ruth swung, struck the ball and then watched it soar over the very spot his foretelling gesture had just predicted. The Yankees won the game and the legend that was Babe Ruth grew.

Now, if Ruth had struck out, we wouldn't be talking about this story. We would be talking about Lou Gehrig, who like Ruth, hit a home run the very next at bat. It's not much of a story if someone claimed to hit a home run and then struck out. It's only a great story because he made a commitment and followed through.

Jesus pointed to something as well. It wasn't a home run; it was an empty tomb. He pointed to the fact that He would rise from the dead, and He did. Matthew 16:21 serves as a turning point, "From that time on, Jesus began to explain to His disciples that He must go to Jerusalem and suffer many things at the hands of the elders, the chief priests and the teachers of the law, and that He must be killed and on the third day be raised to life." These were Jesus' commitments, and He would fulfill each one.

Jesus tells us that all authority has been given to Him (Matt. 28:16-20). We have no reason to doubt that Jesus is fully credentialed and perfectly able to call upon Heaven as we are sent out. His call on our life is directly connected to His commitment to being the authority of God in and through us as we make disciples. We can trust this commitment.

In the same manner, we can fully trust His commitment to be with us – always. Jesus never failed His disciples with His presence. He was with them when everyone was hungry (Matt. 14), when storms raged (Matt. 14), when they got it right and even when they got it wrong (Matt. 16:13-23). His commitment to be present with them was unwavering, and so is His commitment to us.

COMMITMENT ALWAYS OVERRULES COMFORT.

Far too often, we make life decisions based on what makes us most comfortable. But if we are going to say yes to being sent, our commitment to Jesus must overrule our need to be comfortable. For Jesus, resisting the temptation of Satan must not have been comfortable (Matt. 4). It wasn't comfortable for Jesus when He was rejected in His hometown (Matt. 13), and it must have been difficult for Jesus to have to defend Himself against the Pharisees (Matt. 19). The cross certainly wasn't comfortable for Jesus (Matt. 27). His commitment to His Father led Him into each of these situations. Was it always comfortable? No, not even close. Was it fruitful? Beyond what we can even imagine.

My friend, John, was walking through his house one day and he noticed a sign hung on his teenage son's door that read, "No Trespassing, Keep Out!" How often do I put this sign up in the rooms of my life? How often do I shut Jesus out because I don't want Him to come in and see what is really going on? On another occasion, my wife and I were given concert badges that read, "VIP All Access." This is the sign the Lord is looking for His disciples to hang on their hearts. Nothing is off-limits. Nothing is hidden. Will this lead to some discomfort? Yes. However, it's the life that leads to the greatest adventures with the Lord. It's the life of a disciple.

Until commitment overrules comfort, the renewal and revival that
we long to see will remain dreams instead of realities. Comfort leads
to a slumbering faith, whereas commitment leads to a contagious
faith. I think of Peter who received a vision from the Lord in Acts 10.
The Lord sent Peter to Cornelius' house. Peter, a Jewish man, was
called by God to step into the house of a Gentile. This was unheard
of. Yet, Peter says yes. He breaks the threshold of hundreds of years
of division. He preaches the Gospel to a hungry people. Through this
obedience and willingness to be uncomfortable, the entire landscape of Christianity is changed forever. The Lord wants to change
the landscape again. And it happens when we say yes to being sent.

SAYING YES TO BEING SENT INVITES THE POWER OF GOD.

In Matthew 28:18, Jesus tells His disciples that He has been given
"all authority in Heaven and on earth." Nothing is out of the reach of
Jesus. He can do "immeasurably more than all we ask or imagine"
(Eph. 3:20). I'm not a very good poker player – probably a good thing
as a pastor. However, sometimes when I play cards with my family, I
look at my cards and think I have nothing. Then I lay down my hand
and discover, embarrassingly, that I could have won. Sometimes I
forget about what I have in my hand. This is so true in my spiritual
life as well. Sometimes I forget what I carry around every day. We are
empowered by the Spirit of God. This is the Spirit of Jesus, who has
made His home within us. This is the same Jesus who has been given
all authority in Heaven and earth. We do not go about our mission
empty-handed.

If we want to see the power of God, we need to embrace the call of being sent. Radical obedience invites the power of God. 2 Chronicles 16:9 says, "For the eyes of the Lord range throughout the earth to strengthen those whose hearts are fully committed to Him." When our hearts are fully committed to Him, the Lord empowers us to usher in His Kingdom. A partnership with the Lord happens when we step into our call to be the hands and feet of Jesus.

We have a great hand. Now we just need the courage to play it.

SERVE AND ANNOUNCE.

When Jesus sends the 72, He tells them exactly what to do. They were to, "Heal the sick who are there and tell them, 'The Kingdom of God has come near to you'" (Luke 10:9). The Greek word for heal is therapeuein. It denotes serving as well as healing. And the Greek word for sick is asthenes, which also means weakness or inability. Therefore, verse 9 should not be limited to medical cures, but to serving people in their broader needs. To be sent means to serve.

To bring strength to those who are weak.

To help those who are in need.

To bring healing.

To be sent also means to announce. The clear call is to tell people, "The Kingdom of God has come near to you." The thing Jesus wanted announced was that the presence of God had come. He wanted people to know God was here. He wanted everyone to know the King had come. This defines our mission as we are sent. We are called to serve and to announce the presence of God.

WHAT DO YOU WANT TO DO TODAY?

One Saturday morning, I was down in our living room reading when one of my daughters, Reese, came and climbed onto my lap. She cuddled with me for a moment and then asked, "What do you want to do today Papa?" I loved that question. She didn't come and tell me where she wanted to go. Instead, she wanted to know where I wanted to take her.

This really challenged me to go to the Lord and ask the same question. Where do you want to go today Jesus? Where do you want to take me? Where are you sending me?

How about you? Where does God want to send you today?

SECTION 3

SAY YES IN EVERY SEASON!

"My times are in your hands." **PSALM 31:15**

As a New Englander, I know all about seasons. There are seasons of warmth and seasons of cold. I'm either on my tractor mowing, collecting leaves, pushing snow or spreading seed. Life isn't much different. There are many seasons in life, and each season gives us the opportunity to say yes to the Lord as we face it. As you read this book (If you made it this far, thank you by the way!), you are in a season. It could be a season of waiting, when you have to exercise the often-forgotten muscle called patience. The thing you have been praying for has not yet been answered. The position has not become available. The child has not returned. Saying yes to the Lord in this season is an act of true worship. Or, sadly, it's a season of suffering. You are facing all the why questions your heart can handle. Your pain is no longer a guest; it's a roommate. As hard as it can be, choosing to say yes to the Lord in this season is an act of true worship. Or maybe it's a season of pure celebration. Goals have been met, long-awaited yearnings have finally become reality, or major mile markers have been passed. Saying yes to the Lord in this season is also an act of true worship. This final section challenges us to turn to the Lord in every season of life. On the other side of your yes in your current season, the Lord is ready to meet and minister to you personally and powerfully.

CHAPTER THIRTEEN

THE SEASON OF WAITING

"Then Abraham waited patiently, and he received what God had promised." **HEBREWS 6:15**

I couldn't believe that the Trojan Horse Go-Kart line at the acclaimed Mt. Olympus Water and Theme Park in Wisconsin Dells boasted a one-hour wait time. Who were all these people? And didn't most of them drive a big go-kart to get to the park in the first place? Why the need to drive a much smaller and slower version? My daughter Makenna had her eyes on the checkered flag ever since we arrived, so I promised her I would take the ride. We stood in the sun for over 30 minutes before we even made it under the first-century canopy. We zigzagged a hundred times, thinking we had reached the end of the line at each zig, just to realize another zag had begun. But you know what? I loved it.

I didn't love it because I had finally fulfilled my childhood dreams of winning a go-kart race. Honestly, I didn't even care if I beat Makenna around the track.

It's worth noting that I won. By a full lap.

It wasn't the ride that I loved; it was the wait. Yes, the wait was hot and uncomfortable. We felt like cattle being corralled. And I did get kicked about 50 times by a kid who was swinging back and forth on the bars in the queue. When focusing on all the challenges, none of this sounds like much fun, but Makenna was with me, and that's why I loved it. I had an uninterrupted hour to talk, laugh and joke with my daughter.

As a father, the waiting was one of my favorite parts.

Today, we don't like to wait for anything. We want our meals fast, our cars fast and the results of our diets fast as well. If it won't happen quickly, we move on to something faster. Patience is a lost art and tarrying has been long forgotten. If you need to look up the word tarry right now ... I'll wait.

Yet, for our heavenly Father, the waiting is one of His favorite parts. Are you in a season of waiting? A season where you need to exercise the much-avoided gift of patience?

Are you waiting for your next assignment?

Are you waiting for the answer to your prayer?

Are you waiting for a companion?

Are you waiting for a response?

Are you waiting for breakthrough?

Are you waiting for an opportunity?

Are you waiting for healing?

In this season of waiting, will you turn to the Lord? We often want to be on the other side of the problem. Beyond the uncertainty. Enjoying the outcome. Yet, God is with us in it all, and the season of waiting becomes a great moment to draw close to the Lord.

When I think of worshipping the Lord, I often think of a stop light. There is a red light. We worship the Lord when we stop doing the things that keep us from Him. This might mean putting an end to the unhealthy relationship or getting rid of the bad habit. When we say goodbye to the things in our life that keep us from God, our lives become more in tune with Him, which brings Him glory. There is a green light. We can worship God by going where He calls us. When we move out in obedience, it pleases the Lord. The yellow light is often overlooked, sometimes in our lives and always in our driving. There are times when it is best for us to slow down and be patient. We can worship the Lord as we draw close to Him in a season of being still and waiting. Before the answer comes and the challenge is overcome, we can turn to Him in worship. This is not a season of inactivity – but instead one that can launch us into spiritual vibrancy.

GOING IN DEBT

Refusing to be patient costs us. ValuePenguin.com reports that the average credit card debt of U.S. households in 2020 is approximately $5,700, according to the most recent data from the Survey of Consumer Finances by the U.S. Federal Reserve. When we want something, we purchase it before practicing patience, and we quickly find ourselves buried in debt.

Not only do we become financially in debt, but our relationships slip into debt through the disappearance of patience as well. Without patience, we become reactionary. Without prayer and thought, we hurt one another deeply and find ourselves having to dig ourselves out from underneath toxic words and actions that cause significant pain. If we had just practiced patience, we could have avoided the hefty tab.

We would have never sent the text.

We would have never gossiped behind their back.

We would have never compromised their character.

The same is true in our spiritual lives. If we race through a season of waiting, we can find ourselves in debt. As a hockey player, I remember my coach before a game saying, "One minute on and one minute off." This meant that he wanted us to skate hard for one minute and then come back to the bench for a minute of rest. Without the rest, we were useless. In the waiting, we renewed our strength.

The prophet Isaiah says, "but they who wait for the Lord shall renew their strength; they shall mount up with wings like eagles; they shall run and not be weary; they shall walk and not faint" (Isaiah 40:31 ESV). A season of waiting becomes a wonderful opportunity to draw close to the Lord. But when we push through the season without learning and gleaning what we require, we find ourselves spiritually in debt, worn out, weak, wounded and often completely out of alignment.

A LEARNING OPPORTUNITY

There are some things that you can only learn in a season of waiting. Through patience, we learn that God is faithful. When we are willing to wait on the things of God and trust His timing, we learn that He is faithful and trustworthy. Embracing a season of waiting reveals the power of God. When we run ahead on our own, we try to do things in our own strength and understanding. But when we welcome a season of waiting, we experience the power and wisdom of God. We learn that God knows what is best for our lives. But too often we push through seasons of waiting and miss out on the things God had in mind for us. When we sidestep patience, we miss the mighty things God wants to do in and through us.

THE GOD OF THE PROCESS

My friend Gregg always talks about how God is the God of the process. I really like that description because it complements the idea that God never leaves us nor forsakes us. He walks with us in and through everything. Not only that, but He uses the process to mold and shape us. Often, we only go to God when we need something, but He views the journey with us more valuable than the solution.

He wants to walk with you in the illness.

He wants to walk with you in the struggle.

He wants to walk with you in the question.

It's not just about the answer. For God, it's about the journey; it's about the relationship. We are all in process, and He is the God of the process.

THE NATURAL DELAY

There is always a natural delay between planting and harvesting. I remember when Becca and I set up our first garden with our kids. We dug up a patch of our backyard and then planted several different vegetable seeds. We would water the seeds each day and search for any evidence of life. Our kids became frustrated because day after day they didn't see any growth. Nothing was happening — so they thought. Under the surface, the seeds were breaking loose. In the season of waiting, we watered the seeds and uprooted any weeds that emerged. We weren't lazy or inactive. Eventually plants began to emerge in the right timing. This is true in our spiritual lives as well. We plant seeds, water and weed, and then must be patient to see them grow.

Keep praying.

Keep meeting with friends.

Keep listening.

Keep going.

WAITING LEADS TO GOD'S POWER

If you don't want to wait, that's fine. You can move in your own power. But if you choose to wait on His timing, you get to see the power of God.

The gates into the city of Jericho were barricaded completely. No one was able to go in or out. The Lord called on Joshua to intervene with an unconventional battle plan. He gathered the army and marched around the city one time for six days in a row. The priests were sent out to go in front of the Ark of the Covenant, carrying and playing their trumpets along the way. They would do a lap and then return to camp. Then on the seventh day, as commanded, they marched around the city seven times. On the seventh lap, Joshua ordered the army to shout and the walls crumbled.

Imagine you were in the army and it's day four. For the past three days, you marched around the city. You heard the priests playing their trumpets. None of them were playing the same tune, like my high school marching band. It was just a loud noise. Everyone returned to camp and you heard Joshua say, "Same place, same time tomorrow, everyone."

What if the army said, "This is getting old. Let me know how it goes. I'll pray for you." Or even worse, "Let's take the gates ourselves." Instead, they trusted the Lord's timing. Because they were willing to be patient and wait on the Lord, they saw His mighty power.

Are you in a season of waiting? If so, will you say yes to the Lord's ways and the Lord's timing? When you do, walls fall down.

CHAPTER FOURTEEN

THE SEASON OF SUFFERING

"He will wipe every tear from their eyes. There will be no more death or mourning or crying or pain, for the old order of things has passed away." **REVELATION 21:4**

Everything seemed dark and eerily still as I made the nine-and-a-half-minute drive from my home to church. My mind was racing as I prayed and asked God for wisdom. I knew what I was about to walk into was not going to be easy, and I suspected the parents I was going to meet with were going to ask one of the hardest questions imaginable.

"Why did this happen?"

I didn't have the answer. I could give a trite classroom response, but I didn't have the words to satisfy the hearts of the parents whose children were killed in one of the most horrendous school shootings in history. I begged God to give me the answer — but it did not come. I had nothing.

I didn't know why it happened.

I didn't know why God didn't intervene.

My heart was absolutely shattered.

As I drove up to the church building, I sensed the Lord telling me to simply listen, and He would give me the words to share at the right moment. I sat and listened as the parents shared their heartbreaking stories. We cried together. We prayed together. And then one of the parents looked at me and said, "We do have one question for you."

I wasn't ready.

I didn't want them to ask it.

I felt like I was about to throw up.

With love and sincerity in her eyes, she asked, "I know we may never understand why this happened, but how do we move forward?"

I was amazed by the question. They were looking for counsel on how to walk with God in the struggle. We talked about what it means to say yes to the Lord in suffering. We spoke about how walking with the Lord in the hurt and pain would be the way to restored peace, hope and joy. It would not be an easy journey, but it would be better to walk with the Lord than to go without Him.

Seven years later, these parents still don't have the answers to the "Why" question, but they do have amazing stories of God's goodness to them as they continue to walk with Him. This chapter will not answer the "Why" question but instead speak to the "How." How do we walk with the Lord in seasons of suffering? What does it mean to say yes to the Lord in times of trouble?

STRONG IN THE STRUGGLE

As we read Scripture, we encounter people who remained strong in the struggle. Moses faced many challenges, yet he faithfully called upon the Lord. On one occasion, the Lord told Moses that He would send the Israelites into the Promised Land, but He would not go with them because time and time again they had rejected Him. Disappointed and saddened, Moses said to the Lord, "If your Presence does not go with us, do not send us up from here" (Exodus 33:15). Living in the Promised Land without God would be more painful than living in the tough circumstances of the wilderness with God. Without God, they would lose their identity, and this would be too high a price. Moses knew that their strength came from the presence of God.

The story of Job is about a man who lost everything yet remained committed to the Lord. All his friends let him down, those closest to him died, and he lost everything he owned. Job had nothing left but his relationship with the Lord, which was the one thing that brought him hope. Job knew that his strength came from clinging to the Lord.

Acts Chapter 16 records the story of Paul and Silas, who were wrongly accused, beaten and thrown into prison. This would be a difficult situation for any human being, but Paul and Silas remained strong in the Lord. How would you have reacted in this situation?

Would you be upset?

Would you fall into deep sorrow?

Would you blame God?

All these would be reasonable responses. Yet Paul and Silas are found in prison singing praise songs. They did not allow the trial to interrupt their relationship with the Lord. Instead, they saw it as an opportunity to see the power of God. Even though they were in shackles, they weren't going to give up on God. Could it be that their confidence in the Lord led them to believe their situation was simply a great opportunity for God to do something remarkable? Of this event, early Christian author Tertullian said, "The legs feel nothing in the stocks when the heart is in Heaven."

Despite their circumstances, each of these people continually said yes to the Lord. Their outlook was not determined by their situation or circumstances but was rooted in the Lord. When our identities are strongly placed in the Lord, we can weather any storm. Even when times are difficult, we can know the healing and comforting presence of our King.

LOOK IN THE DIRECTION YOU WANT TO GO

I bought a motorcycle before I knew how to ride one. It was embarrassing having to ask the sales guy to ride my newly purchased 1979 Suzuki GS850 to my house for me while I safely followed him in my earth-tone, four-door Saturn sedan. I eventually took a three-day motorcycle course to earn the accredited "M" on my driver's license. One of the major lessons learned from the course, besides learning that pretty much anyone can get a motorcycle license, was learning how to best turn the bike. It's not as simple as turning the wheel in a car. You must lean and look. The best way to get the motorcycle to go in the direction you want is by looking in the direction you want to go. Where you turn your head, your body will naturally lean and the bike will follow.

The same is true in a season of suffering. When we keep our eyes on the Lord and look to Him, we will be drawn into His presence. Through His presence, we will know His peace and comfort. So, how do we look to Jesus in the struggle?

- Spend time in His Word.

- Take a walk with Him in prayer.

- Commit to worshipping in a church community.

- Invest in helpful fellowship.

- Look for opportunities to serve others.

Lean into these and let them lead you into the presence of the Lord. Intentionally look in the direction you want to go.

LET PEOPLE IN

As a pastor, I have heard many stories of people walking through all kinds of trials. A critical component of most of these stories is the help and love of trusted friends. It can be very difficult to allow people into your suffering, but it is necessary. You may feel like you are burdening the friend with your trial; however, when friends are invited into your struggle, it can bring a sense of purpose for them. Good friends want to help. Allow others to shoulder some of the weight of your pain. Jesus received help in the struggle as Simon of Cyrene briefly carried His cross (Matthew 27:32). We too must welcome others to carry our cross.

DON'T WASTE ANYTHING

Much like there are some things that we can only learn through patience, there are also some things that we can only learn through suffering.

We can learn valuable lessons through our suffering about how to comfort others in their seasons of trial. In 2 Corinthians 1:3-4, Paul writes, "Praise be to the God and Father of our Lord Jesus Christ, the Father of compassion and the God of all comfort, who comforts us in all our troubles, so that we can comfort those in any trouble with the comfort we ourselves receive from God." We can learn about the strength, power and trustworthiness of God through seasons of struggle. Experiencing the promised presence of God in the storm strengthens our confidence in the promise that He will never leave nor forsake us (Hebrews 13:5). Each of these lessons becomes valuable when helping others through their seasons of suffering.

No matter where the trials come from, there are lessons that can be learned. A good friend of mine who has been in a cancer battle told me, "Brian, if I'm going to go through all the pain of this battle, I'm going to make it count." I've watched as he has made the most of every situation. He has ministered to the doctors and nursing staff. He has supported countless others going through their own cancer battles. And he has spoken to churches, businesses and leaders about the valuable lessons he has gained in the struggle. Nothing has gone to waste.

DON'T BELIEVE THE LIES

Many questions accompany seasons of suffering. When attempting to satisfy these questions, we can easily adopt answers that are both untrue and unhelpful. It's very important to sort through what is true and what is false. Maybe you've been told:

· You are suffering because of your poor choices.

· You are suffering because of someone else's poor choices.

It's possible that our suffering was brought on by our own poor choices. If I choose to keep bad company, I shouldn't be surprised if bad things happen from those relationships. If you choose to reach out to the high school crush through social media, then you shouldn't be surprised when you're led down an unhealthy path. But this doesn't apply to all suffering. Your trial might have nothing to do with your personal choices but instead are the result of the broken-ness of this world. It may not be the outcome of someone else's poor choices either. These two statements can be true; however, when applied without merit, they become very unhelpful and only lead to unnecessary heartache.

Or maybe you have been told:

- You are suffering because God is getting back at you for your past sin.

- God must not be with you because you are suffering.

- God must not love you because you are suffering.

- You must not trust God because you are still suffering.

These statements are never true. We cannot believe these lies. Our God is not a revenge God looking for an opportunity to get back at us for sin from our past. When we turn to Him, our sins are forgiven. He does not hold onto a record to throw in your face at the opportune time. Our God is also always with us. He does not leave us, and we often experience His closeness most tangibly in times of trouble. Suffering does not mean He no longer loves us or that we lack trust.

When we hold onto these lies, they lead to a false understanding of who God is – and they result in a watered-down version of God's grace, mercy and power.

We need to be reminded of the truth in our suffering. We have a God who very much loves us. We have a God who will walk with us. We live in a world that is broken. There is an evil one who prowls around like a lion looking to devour us. Yet, in the end, our God will be victorious. Even in the suffering, we can find our hope in the Lord.

It's one thing to say to an accomplished skydiving instructor, "You are an amazing skydiving instructor. No one compares to your skydiving ways. All praise to you mighty skydiving instructor." It's another thing entirely to jump with him.

We can say, "God you are amazing. There is no one like you. You comfort the brokenhearted. You draw near to the hurting." But walking in a season of suffering with the Lord is jumping with Him.

When we choose to say yes to the Lord in a season of suffering – we jump. And in the jumping, we experience firsthand His peace, His comfort and His hope.

CHAPTER FIFTEEN

THE SEASON OF CELEBRATION

"Rejoice in the Lord always. I will say it again: Rejoice!"

PHILIPPIANS 4:4

In his commentary on the Gospel of Luke, Bruce Larson shared a story about a conference that was held at a Presbyterian church in Omaha. Each person was given a red helium-filled balloon to release at any point during the service to express their great joy in the Lord. Everyone loved this creative idea — except the facilities team. Throughout the service, balloons ascended into the rafters of the church as a beautiful picture of celebration. At the end of the service, two-thirds of the balloons covered the ceiling of the building. As for the other one-third, they remained in the hands of the participants who found no reason to celebrate.

How could this be?

For the Christian, there are always reasons to celebrate. We can find joy amid a season of waiting and even in a season of suffering. Paul, who was no stranger to suffering, wrote, "We rejoice in our sufferings" (Romans 5:3, ESV). There should always be a reason for followers of Jesus to release the red helium-filled balloon. Jesus Himself prayed, "I am coming to you now, but I say these things while I am still in the world, so that they may have the full measure of my joy within them" (John 17:13). Jesus wants us to experience a joy that leads to a life of celebration.

I'm not sure whether my church likes it or not, but I often tell them we need to party more. We need to relearn how to celebrate. We can't have one-third of us still holding onto our balloons. We should pursue a life of celebration that becomes a part of every season.

MANY BRANDS OF JOY

Joy must be expressed. Like water, joy always finds a way out. Where there is a problem celebrating, there is a shortage of joy. Pastor Jack Wellman defines joy as "an emotion that's acquired by the antici-pation, acquisition or even the expectation of something great or wonderful." So, what great and wonderful thing are you anticipating, have you acquired or are you expecting? That great and wonderful thing will determine the extent of your joy and ultimately the degree of your celebration.

Is it an upcoming wedding?

Is it the completion of a degree you have been working on?

Is it a new position?

Is it finding the man or woman of your dreams?

Is it a home on the lake?

What is your great and wonderful thing? I must warn you at this point that there are different brands of joy, and they are not all equal. King Solomon went after the things he thought would bring happiness. Yet, what he found was a fleeting joy. He gave his heart to many things, but they all left him empty. David, on the other hand, called on the Lord to fill his heart with joy (Psalm 4:7). For David, the great and wonderful thing was God Himself.

Where you find joy and happiness is a daily choice, and there are many brands out there vying for you to purchase them. Throughout the pages of Scripture, we learn of the dangers of chasing after counterfeit joy. In Psalm 20, David says, "Some trust in chariots and some in horses, but we trust in the name of the Lord our God." I don't know about you, but I've never trusted in chariots. In fact, I don't own a single chariot, unless David prophetically intended to include a 2010 silver Honda Odyssey. Yet, this does not mean this passage doesn't apply to us today.

We trust in our ways over God's ways.

We trust in our understanding over God's wisdom.

We trust in our feelings over God's desires.

We trust in our plans over God's mission.

When we trust in things lower than what God has to offer, it leads us to a counterfeit joy. It's not the real thing. We must resist the brands of joy and celebration that find their source in things less than God.

REASONS TO CELEBRATE

In Luke Chapter 2, we read the story of Jesus' birth. One of my favorite parts about Luke's telling of this story is that the first people to know about Jesus' birth, besides Mary and Joseph, were the shepherds. They were the most unlikely group of people to be told about the Messiah being born. Why didn't God send the angel to announce the birth to Mary's parents first? I thought that was common courtesy. This was a calculated announcement. On the very first day of Jesus' life, God was already announcing the kind of Kingdom He came to establish. It was one that would be open to all people — even shepherds.

Even me.

Even you.

The shepherds were conducting business as usual when suddenly an angel of the Lord appeared before them. Then the angel spoke words of truth that should cause us all to be in a perpetual posture of celebration.

"Do not be afraid."

The angel did not want the shepherds to miss the message because of their fear of the situation. This can happen to us as well. Our joy is robbed by fear. God is always offering us great joy in Him, yet it gets drowned out by fear.

Fear of missing out.

Fear of what others think.

Fear of not being good enough.

Fear of not being loved.

In Jesus, we have no reason to fear these things. When we are with Jesus, we are never missing out. When we know what the Lord thinks of us, what others think becomes secondary. When we know Jesus, we are ok with our own weaknesses because in Him we are made strong. We are empowered by the Holy Spirit. And we know, because of all that God has done for us, that we are His beloved children. In Jesus, all fear melts away. Scripture teaches us that "perfect love drives out fear" (1 John 4:18). Not only do we have no reason to fear, but we also have the love of Jesus that drives out fear. These all seem like good reasons to celebrate daily.

"I bring you good news."

Have you ever been given news that lifted your spirits? I'm sure all of us can remember times when good news changed our outlook and gave us new perspective. News can affect us both positively and negatively.

Have you ever heard someone say, "No news is good news"? I'm not a fan of this phrase because it implies that the only news, we are getting is bad news. Therefore, when we are not receiving any news, that means all things are good in the world. "If I can just keep things as they are, I will be happy." I think we should revolt against this kind of thinking. I don't want "no news is good news." I want good news to be good news. We don't need the absence of news to be good news, because we have wonderfully amazing news.

We should be continually celebrating that the Lord brought good news, "The Savior – yes, the Messiah, the Lord – has been born." We have a Savior who has paid for our sin, welcomed us in His presence and opened Heaven's gates. I'd say these are all reasons to celebrate.

THE PATH TO CELEBRATION

While in Jerusalem before Jesus' death on the cross, an expert in the law asked Jesus, "Teacher, which is the greatest commandment in the law" (Matthew 22:36)? The answer Jesus would give tells us how to thrive as His followers. If we are going to live a life filled with the joy of the Lord, then we must follow Jesus' answer. These words are possibly the most important in all of Scripture. Jesus responds by saying, "'Love the Lord your God with all your heart and with all your soul and with all your mind.' This is the first and greatest commandment. And the second is like it: 'Love your neighbor as yourself.' All the Law and the Prophets hang on these two commandments" (Matthew 22:37-40). A life of celebration is found on the other side of our yes to these two great commands.

The path to celebration is paved by obeying the Lord. This is what it means to love Him. In his book "Celebration of Discipline," Richard Foster says, "In the spiritual life only one thing will produce genuine joy, and that is obedience. The old hymn tells us that there is no other way to be happy in Jesus but to 'trust and obey.'" We don't have to over spiritualize obedience. Pining over how to be obedient is not necessary. You don't have to have 30 years of following the Lord under your belt to know how to obey Him. It does not require a degree in Greek. The Lord has clearly told us what to do in His Word.

Forgive.

Be generous.

Praise the Lord.

Meet the needs of the most vulnerable.

Study His Word.

Pray and fast.

Be kind, patient and gentle.

Be strong and courageous.

Be filled with His Spirit.

Make disciples.

When we obey these things, we place ourselves right at the core of who we are called to be as God's children, and God meets us there. Doing these things does not define our faith. But doing these things strengthens our relationship with the one who does – Jesus. And when we strengthen our relationship with Jesus, it leads to joy. And joy leads to a life of celebration.

I love how the expert in law asks Jesus for the greatest command-ment, and Jesus precedes to give him two. You can never put Jesus into a box. The second command is like the first, "Love your neighbor as yourself." Our creator wants us to honor and love His created ones. When we do, it leads to joy. But for some reason, this is not easy for us. We struggle with others because we constantly compare our-selves to everyone else. We do things to make sure we are on top.

We gossip.

We lie.

We play favorites.

We have not had a successful record as humankind when it comes to loving our neighbor. This must change. And the only way it will is through the filling of the Spirit. On our own we are unable to love others with the love of Christ. The sooner we realize and accept this, the sooner we can become something different.

My daughter Norah decided to run for office to be on the third grade Student Council. Becca and I worked on her speech, because if a Mowrey is going to give a speech, it is going to be well-thought-out and well-rehearsed. She was 9 at the time so she came up with nine reasons why her classmates should vote for her. She practiced the speech and was ready to go.

Election day came and Norah went to school dressed for success. When the bus pulled up after school, Norah came leaping off with a smile stretching from ear to ear. She ran to Becca, who was waiting for her on the porch, and said with great excitement, "Guess what Mama!"

"Did you win?" Becca asked.

"No," she said, still smiling.

Norah then went on to tell Becca that there were two spots on the Student Council. The first spot went to a boy named Matthew.

"But don't worry Mama," Norah said. "Matthew is going to do a great job. Everyone likes Matthew. But guess what?"

Becca, thinking Norah had good news to share, said, "So you got the second spot!"

"No," said Norah, still with a smile on her face. "Jake got the second spot. And he will be great. He goes to our church. But there's more Mama."

Norah then told Becca that there was a backup spot, just in case one of the Student Council members could not fulfill their judiciary responsibilities.

"So, you are the back up," Becca assumed.

"No," said Norah enthusiastically. "Sarah is the back up. And Mama, she is going to do so good. She is a great artist." "But guess what Mama? I'm the back up to the back up."

Struggling to grasp why Norah was so pleased with this accomplishment, Becca replied, "That's awesome Norah. I'm so proud of you. Just out of curiosity, how many kids ran for office?"

Full of joy, Norah looked at Becca and proudly said, "Four!"

Becca and I were confused, but we had never been prouder. Norah was so happy for everyone else, and this brought her great joy. She possesses something within her that is God-given — a special love for others that reaches past her desire to promote herself.

There is always a reason to celebrate. It just might not be your reason. When we learn to celebrate the successes and achievements of others, we will step into a more joy-filled life. After washing His disciples' feet, Jesus turned to His disciples and said, "I have set you an example that you should do as I have done for you" (John 13:15). This is how we are to live — looking for opportunities to serve one another. Blessing others leads to a life filled with celebration.

Release your red balloon.

ON THE OTHER SIDE OF YES

STUDY GUIDE

By Brian Mowrey and Tim Washer

My friend Jeff loves to say, "Let's make the most of it." A dinner gone wrong – "Let's make the most of it." Rain on his wedding day – "Let's make the most of it." Gum stuck in his daughter's hair — get out the scissors and "Let's make the most of it."

A book called "On the Other Side of Yes" – "Let's make the most of it."

The way to make the most of this book is by making it personal. Prayer, fasting and generosity are good ideas on their own; however, once applied to your life, they have the potential to transform your life and impact the Kingdom of God. This study guide is here to help you make the things spoken about in this book a reality in your life.

For the overachiever, grab a pen and journal. You will want to reflect on the questions personally and record your own commitments and convictions. Each chapter's study concludes with a "Say Yes Challenge" in bold to help you and your group take next steps.

We also encourage you to invite trusted friends with you on this journey. Connect with a crew of friends, a small group of friends or a community group of friends. Share with one another. Commit to the things God is challenging you to together and pray for one another as you step out and say yes to the Lord.

And then get ready to experience what's on the other side of yes.

CHAPTER ONE
YOU ARE LOVED

1. Have you ever received a gift that was motivated out of obligation? How did it make you feel?

2. Read **JOHN 3:16** and list the five most important features of the passage:

   a) _____

   b) _____

   c) _____

   d) _____

   e) _____

3. The greatest gift we have received is the presence of God in our lives. Why has God given us this gift? What was His motivation?

4. What would it practically look like for you to walk the "length and breadth" of God's love? How do you plan to embrace and experience the love of God fully?

5. Are you carrying around any shame, hurt, failure, guilt or regret that needs to be laid down? Imagine yourself laying it at the cross and walking away. You could even write it down and burn it in a fire or flush it down the toilet (sorry about the potty language).

6. How does the author comment on the width of God's love? Have you experienced God's love in this way?

7. Have you ever loved something and then that love wore out? How does this compare to the love of God?

8. List the times in your life when you have been able to stand on the love of God to help you overcome a trial, struggle or obstacle:

_____

_____

_____

_____

_____

_____

9. What are the four ways Paul described the love of God in **EPHESIANS 3:18**? Discuss with your group how each of these reflects different dimensions of God's love:

a) _____

b) _____

c) _____

d) _____

 SAY YES CHALLENGE ═══════════════════════

Write down **Isaiah 54:10** and post it somewhere you will see it every day for the next week. Memorize the passage and reflect on the love God has for you.

CHAPTER TWO
YOU HAVE A PURPOSE

1. Think back on the experiences of life when you felt the most joy. What were you doing? What gifts were you using? Who was there?

2. Read **1 KINGS 19:1-8**. Have you ever realized you were in the wrong place? How did you know? God came and rescued Elijah from the cave. How did He come to your rescue?

3. According to **EXODUS 8:1**, why does God free His people? How does this relate to our purpose today?

4. If our purpose is to worship the Lord, list the ways you can worship Him in each of these areas:

   a.   With your time

   b.   With your gifts

c.   With your resources

d.   In your relationships

e.   With your attitude

f.   Through service

5. Read **1 CORINTHIANS 12:12-26**. In verse 15, the Apostle Paul says, "If the foot says, 'I'm not part of the body because I am not a hand,' that does not make it any less part of the body." How does this speak to you about your part in the body of Christ? What do we learn about the value of others and their unique contribution to the body?

6. What gifts has God given you? How did you discover them? How have others affirmed these gifts? How are you using them to bless His Kingdom?

7. God doesn't call the equipped; He equips the called. Is this statement true?

8. What purpose is God calling you to right now? In your relationships? In your families? In your neighborhoods? In your schools? In your work? With your gifts and talents?

 SAY YES CHALLENGE

In your journal, write down the place, like Elijah, where you go to hide. Next, write down ways that you can avoid the natural tendency to return to the cave. Finally, describe what it looks like for you to be fully engaged in the things of the Lord.

CHAPTER THREE
YOU ARE NOT ALONE

1. Can you recall a time when you received an invitation that helped pull you out of loneliness? What about the invitation made you feel loved and appreciated?

2. Read **DEUTERONOMY 31:8**. What do you learn about the presence of God?

3. Recall a time where you felt closest to God? What was unique about that season?

4. How do you best experience the presence of God? Is it a place? Is it with certain friends? Is it while in nature? Is it through serving?

5. God is near, He is moving, and He can move through you.

   a. **God Is Near:** Read **1 KINGS 19:9-13**. How did God reveal His presence to Elijah, and why did He do it in this way?

b. **God Is Moving:** To experience the presence of God we need to be connected to His Spirit. How do we keep in step with the Spirit of God? Like the missionary's car in the book, are there any loose connections keeping you from experiencing the full power of God in your life?

c. **God Can Move Through You:** Reflect on the biblical characters who were ordinary people, yet God used to do extraordinary things. Who comes to mind? Now recall a time in your life when you felt unqualified but God used you in a special way.

6. If God is present, He must want to speak to us. How do you hear God? Spend some time asking Him for an encouraging and edifying word for your friends, small group and family right now.

 SAY YES CHALLENGE ══════════════

Over this next week, look for a time to be present with someone who would be blessed by your company. Go and encourage that person and seek the Lord on his or her behalf.

CHAPTER FOUR
SAY YES TO PRAYER

1. How has prayer been important in your life? Has your prayer life
    evolved over time? What is responsible for this evolution?

2. Is praying out of obligation different from praying out of
    relationship? If so, how do you learn to pray from your relationship
    with the Lord? Has there ever been a time in your life when prayer
    has not come easy? What do you think caused this interference?
    What helped you overcome this difficulty?

3. Even the disciples had to learn how to pray. Read **LUKE 11:1**. What do
    you think the disciples saw in Jesus that they wanted? What was
    so special?

4. Through prayer, we hear from God. What suggestions does the
    author make to help us hear from God more clearly? How have these
    impacted you?

5. How have you experienced God answering your prayer? Through opening a door? Through closing a door? Through asking you to wait?

6. God can answer our prayers through a "no" or "wait." Why does God sometimes answer in this way?

7. Is there a prayer on your heart that you have not yet prayed? Moving forward, how can you be intentional in your prayer life? How can you make prayer a regular part of your life?

8. Read **MATTHEW 6:5-13**. What lessons can you learn from Jesus about how to pray?

 SAY YES CHALLENGE

Starting today, for the next 20 days, spend the first 20 minutes of your day with Jesus in prayer. Get started at www.walnuthillcc.org/first-20.

CHAPTER FIVE
SAY YES TO FASTING

1. The author says, "Fasting is possibly the most forgotten, misunderstood and sadly avoided gift that God has given us." Why do you believe that is? When you think of fasting, what comes to mind? What is your personal experience with fasting? Was it difficult? Were there any rewards?

2. Read **MATTHEW 9:14-15**. According to Jesus' teaching, when is the time for fasting?

3. Read **1 THESSALONIANS 5:23**. How does fasting reprioritize your life?

4. Have you ever had someone lay something down to be with you or help you? How did that make you feel? In this line of thinking, why is fasting considered worship? What is God calling you to put down as an act of worship? Work? TV? Food? Hobby? Sweets? Drink?

5. Read ISAIAH 58:6-9. How would you describe God's chosen way of
    fasting? How can choosing to fast become a blessing to others?

6. The author proposes that fasting intensifies the power of prayer.
    Reflect on the stories in the Bible where God's people fasted and
    the Lord moved in power (NEHEMIAH 1, EZRA 8:21-23, ESTHER 4:15-16, 2
    SAMUEL 12:14-16, ACTS 10:30, ACTS 13:2-3, ACTS 14:23, MATTHEW 4:1-11).

7. Read Jesus' teaching on fasting from MATTHEW CHAPTER 6, and write
    down or discuss how this can apply to your life today?

 SAY YES CHALLENGE ════════════════════════════

Pray about how God is calling you to fast. Write down your
objective for your time of fasting. Is there a certain question
you want God to answer? Is there an injustice you want to
seek God for? Are you asking for wisdom into a situation?
Once your fast is completed, write down the ways God
specifically spoke to you.

CHAPTER SIX
SAY YES TO FORGIVENESS

1. Have you ever had to ask for forgiveness? What was that like? Was it difficult? What did it lead to? Did it heal the relationship? If not, what did it accomplish within you?

2. Sometimes it seems easier to hold onto the pain than to forgive. Where has this been true in your life?

3. What's the difference between the author's description of "burying the hatchet" and Pastor Thomas Watson's definition of forgiveness: "When we strive against all thoughts of revenge; when we will not do our enemies harm, but wish well to them, grieve at their calamities, pray for them, seek reconciliation with them, and show ourselves ready on all occasions to relieve them"?

4. What keeps us from this kind of forgiveness?

5. The author proposes that forgiveness is a choice and restoration is the process. Once we choose to forgive, what does the restoration process look like? Will restoration always be the result of forgiveness?

6. Read **LUKE 6:27-36**. Jesus calls us to love others with an extravagant kind of love. In doing so, He is teaching us to protect our identities in Him. What stands out to you from this passage about what it means to be the children of God?

7. How is forgiveness more for the forgiver than the forgiven?

8. Ask the Lord to reveal the people who you need to forgive. Pray also for God to reveal the people you need to ask forgiveness from.

 SAY YES CHALLENGE

For the next seven days, read **Colossians 3:1-14** and reflect on the gift of God's forgiveness and the call to be people who forgive and love one another.

CHAPTER SEVEN
SAY YES TO PEACEMAKING

1. Would you see yourself more as a reactor or a responder? What are the benefits and costs of both?

2. Read **LUKE 10:1-9**. What do you learn about the world you live in, and what do you learn about how you are to respond?

3. Being a good peacemaker takes practice. What are some ways to practice being a good peacemaker?

4. Peace is not the absence of conflict or disagreement. If that is the case, how do you carry peace into situations of conflict and disagreement?

5. Describe the difference between hearing and listening. How does this help with your posture of being a peacemaker?

6. Read **1 PETER 5:7** and reflect on the ways you can cast your fears on the Lord and be a carrier of His peace.

7. Peace is always under attack. How does starting your day with Jesus help you remain rooted in your call to be a peacemaker?

8. When have you worked toward peace but couldn't achieve it? When have you experienced great conflict that surprisingly resolved itself peacefully? How have you seen God in both?

 SAY YES CHALLENGE ═══════════════

What steps can you take to become more of a responder than a reactor? Write down specific ways you intend to practice being a peacemaker. Seek the Lord for a word of encouragement that would bring someone peace.

CHAPTER EIGHT
SAY YES TO COMPASSION

1. Have you ever experienced an act of compassion that stopped you in your tracks? How did it impact you?

2. Have you ever heard God described in these ways:

   a. Judge

   b. Angry

   c. Absent

   d. A Holy Santa Claus

   e. Magic Lamp God

   f. Loving

   g. Compassionate

3. Read **2 CORINTHIANS 1:3-4**. Have you ever wondered if your mistake or failure was covered by God's grace? God has compassion on all people for all things. Do you reflect the same kind of compassion to others? If not, what gets in the way?

4. Compassion is incomplete without action. When have you
    modeled this? What was the impact on you and others?

5. The author describes compassion as seeing, feeling and moving.
    How do you see this in the story of the Prodigal Son? In which of
    these do you excel? In which do you need to grow?

6. List the times when Jesus showed compassion to the most
    vulnerable. What can you learn from His ministry of compassion?

 SAY YES CHALLENGE ══════════════════════════

Compassion always has a who attached to it. Who is the Lord
placing on your heart to show compassion toward? This week,
write them a note, meet their need, drop off a meal, and sit
and listen to their story.

CHAPTER NINE
SAY YES TO UNITY

1. Can you recall a time when you belonged to a community that made you feel like family? What was unique about this experience?

2. Read **JOHN 17** and list all the things Jesus prayed for:

   _____

   _____

   _____

   _____

3. What is the difference between getting along and unity?

4. Write a short definition of biblical unity.

5. What barriers keep you from the kind of unity Jesus prays for? What is missing in our world that has caused such significant fractures among us?

6. Read **EPHESIANS 4:1-6**. Why does unity depend on the Holy Spirit?

7. Which of the nine commitments from the chapter connected with you in the most meaningful or convicting way? Why?

 SAY YES CHALLENGE ═══════════════════════

Work through the nine commitments addressed in the chapter and write down how you plan to personally commit to each of them.

CHAPTER TEN
SAY YES TO GRATITUDE

1. When the author was in high school, he was on the golf team. During one match, his opponent hit a hole in one. You would think the young golfer would have been over the moon, but he simply picked up his golf tee and walked to retrieve his ball without any reaction. Can you remember a time when someone's response to an event or gift was underwhelming in comparison to what they received?

2. Read **LUKE 17:11-19**. Why was the one leper commended by Jesus? Why do you think the other nine did not return? Is there anything you have received from the Lord for which you still need to thank Him?

3. Johann Sabastian Bach would always sign his pieces with the inscription SDG for Soli Deo Gloria, which means glory to God alone. His intent was to give God all the glory for his work, believing that it was not his accomplishments but God's masterful work done through him. What would it look like for you to mark every area of your life with SDG? Your home? Your workplace? Your relationships?

4. According to the author, why is gratitude important? Which of these benefits resonates with you personally?

5. Read **PSALM 100:4**. What does it mean to you to enter His gates with thanksgiving?

6. Gratitude doesn't happen by accident. List several ways you can become a more thankful person?

7. If you are in a group, have each person share a word of thanks for one other member of the group. For those of you reading individually, write a letter of thanks to a friend or family member.

 SAY YES CHALLENGE ════════════════════════

Every night this week, give thanks to the Lord for five things. Write them down. Each night, reflect on the previous night's list.

CHAPTER ELEVEN
SAY YES TO GENEROSITY

1. Have you ever been the recipient of someone else's generosity? What did it mean to you? And what did you learn from it? How did it impact your generosity?

2. Why is generosity often difficult? Has there been a time in your life when you struggled to be generous? What were the reasons?

3. The author shared three barriers to generosity from the story of the rich young ruler. What are those barriers, and which resonate most with you?

4. Read **2 CORINTHIANS 9:6-15**. How have you known these principles to be true:

   a.   You reap what you sow.

   b.   Giving is a matter of the heart.

   c.   Give cheerfully.

   d.   God is trustworthy.

   e.   God is the source.

   f.   Giving is partnership.

5. Read **MALACHI 3:10**. What is the command of this passage? What is the promise in this passage? (Extra Credit: Find any other place in Scripture where God says, "Test me in this.")

6. Recall a time in your life when your generosity led to breakthrough and blessing?

7. Remembering the things you are grateful for from the past chapter, which of these things could you regift to the Lord? Are there any other areas of your life that could be regifted back to the Lord? Your gifts? Your resources? Your time?

 SAY YES CHALLENGE ═══════════════════

Write out your generosity plan. How will you intentionally be generous? Open up your home to fellowship with others. Give rides to those in need. Commit to regularly giving financially to benefit God's Kingdom.

CHAPTER TWELVE
SAY YES TO BEING SENT

1. What does it mean to be Christian? Is there a person in your life who reflects this kind of life?

2. If we want the most fulfilling life, we must embrace our mission as the sent ones of God. Do you agree with this statement? Why or why not?

3. The author speaks about the story of Ruth. She could have gone back to her hometown but instead chooses to follow Naomi. She was fully committed to her mother-in-law. Scripture says that "Ruth clung" to Naomi. What are the things you are tempted to cling to when facing the choice to radically follow the Lord?

4. List the reasons Christians can have complete confidence in the Lord as His sent ones. What are the reasons you can trust Him fully?

5. Read **LUKE 10:9**. What is our mission to the world? Can you think of any other passages in Scripture that give us our marching orders as the body of Christ?

6. Recall a time when the Lord called you to a mission. How did you know He was calling you? Did He equip you for the call? How did you see God move as you stepped out in faith? Remember to write these things down.

 SAY YES CHALLENGE ══════════════════

Each day this week in your First 20, ask the Lord, "Where do you want to go today, Lord? Where do you want to send me?" As you listen to the Lord, write down what you hear and then follow through on what He calls you to.

CHAPTER THIRTEEN
THE SEASON OF WAITING

1. Can you recall when you were in a season of waiting? How did you grow in the Lord? What were the challenges? How did waiting become a blessing?

2. Can you remember a time when you opted for the shortcut? What were the outcomes? Can you think of a time in the Bible when a person went ahead of the Lord without His blessing? How did that work out?

3. How does refusing to be patient hurt you?

4. Read **ISAIAH 40:31 (ESV)**. Why does waiting on the Lord bring renewed strength?

5. What lessons can you learn only in a season of waiting?

6. Read **JOHN 11:17-44**. Why was Martha so upset? What was accomplished through Jesus' waiting to visit that could not have happened if He arrived while Lazarus was still alive? Have you ever seen God do something beyond what you could have imagined because of a season of waiting?

7. Share with a friend or your group what you are waiting on the Lord for today. What challenges has this created for you? Spend time together praying for one another.

 SAY YES CHALLENGE ═══════════════════

What is God calling you to persevere in prayer for? Write it down and post it on your mirror as a reminder to pray.

CHAPTER FOURTEEN
THE SEASON OF SUFFERING

1. How have you experienced the presence of God in seasons of suffering?

2. Read **EXODUS 33:12-17**. Why was the presence of God more important to Moses than the blessing of taking the Promised Land?

3. How does a relationship with Jesus help you in your trials?

4. List several ways you can keep your focus on Jesus during seasons of suffering:

_____

_____

_____

_____

_____

5. Read **2 CORINTHIANS 1:3-4**. How do seasons of suffering prepare us to be a blessing to others? What lessons have you learned from your own seasons of suffering? How have you been able to be a source of comfort to others in their season of suffering?

6. What truths can you lean on in seasons of suffering?

7. What suffering are you facing right now? Who can walk with you in it? Share with a trusted friend or with your group.

 SAY YES CHALLENGE ════════════════════

Do a Scripture study and write out the promises of God. Highlight the ones that are particularly timely for you in this season. Write a card to a friend using one of the verses you discovered as a source of encouragement.

CHAPTER FIFTEEN
THE SEASON OF CELEBRATION

1. If you were handed a red helium-filled balloon right now (as spoken about in the chapter), what would you release it for? What is bringing you joy?

2. The author proposed that joy and celebration can be a part of any season of life. Do you believe this is true? How have you experienced joy and celebration in different seasons of life?

3. Has there ever been a time in your life when you were left feeling empty after chasing a counterfeit joy? What were you chasing, and why did it leave you feeling empty?

4. Read LUKE 2:1-15. What do you learn about living a life filled with joy and celebration from the words of the angel?

5. How does fear block you from experiencing joy? What fears keep you from living a life of celebration?

6. Read **MATTHEW 22:34-40**. How do these two great commandments become the path to joy and celebration? How does obedience lead to joy?

7. Share a time when you experienced great joy through loving and serving others?

 SAY YES CHALLENGE ══════════════════════

Throw a party! Invite some friends over and celebrate. Prepare a word for each person who attends. Pray over them and thank the Lord for His goodness in each person's life. Have fun, joke around and maybe even dance.

ACKNOWLEDGMENTS

My greatest adventures have been on the other side of saying yes to the Lord. I'm so grateful for the Lord's faithfulness to me in every season of life.

On the other side of saying yes to writing this book was a team of friends and loved ones who supported and encouraged me every step of the way. Special thanks to my reading team for your insight and wisdom. Tim Washer, Becca Mowrey and Jessica Reinhart, your collaboration on this project was a tremendous help. Immeasurable thanks to you for pouring your heart into this book. On the other side of your yes to being on the reading team was countless hours of hard work. But we had a ton of fun! Let's do it again sometime!

Thank you to Anna Mae Althen for editing the book and more importantly for praying for me through the whole process. To Parker Hu for designing the cover and formatting the content and Connie McFarland for being great at everything you do.

Additional thanks to my good friend Tim Washer for being such a great source of encouragement and always reminding me to celebrate along the way. Thank you for encouraging me to bring humor into the book whenever possible. Unless people don't think the book is funny — then I take back my thanks.

A huge thank you to my Dad and Mom, Ray and Nancy Mowrey, for getting me spelling help in second grade, and for your constant love and support. Much love to my church family at Walnut Hill and special thanks to Adam DePasquale and Craig Mowrey for the joy of leading together. Craig, I need to ask your permission for some of the stories told in this book. Let's grab lunch soon.

To my beautiful girls Makenna, Norah, Reese and Bria. I love you all so much. You are game changers, and I'm so proud of who you are becoming. I am truly blessed to be your Papa.

Finally, to my wonderful wife Becca. I love you. You are the greatest blessing to ever happen to me — hands down.

CONNECT WITH BRIAN

Brian has a heart for equipping and encouraging
leaders and inspiring people through the Word of God.
To arrange a time to speak with Brian about an event
or speaking engagement, or simply to chat about life,
leadership and ministry, you can reach him by emailing
hello@brianmowrey.com. For more resources, visit
www.brianmowrey.com and www.walnuthillcc.org.

Made in the USA
Monee, IL
20 November 2023

46823367R00125